Coming Home to Venus

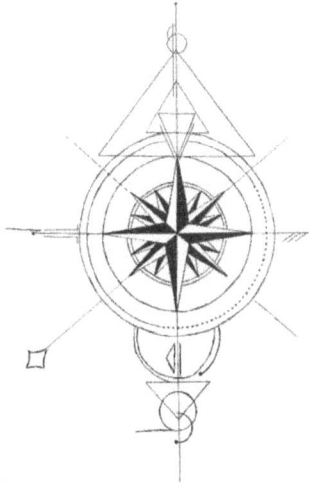

The story of a woman transitioning to her real self

Ella Marques

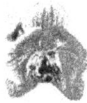

Coral Orchid Press

Coming Home to Venus

Coming Home to Venus

Disclaimer

I have tried to recreate events, locales, and conversations from my memories of them as well as I could. In order to maintain their anonymity, in some instances I have changed the names of individuals, companies, and places. I have also changed some identifying characteristics and details such as physical properties, occupations, and places of residence. Some dialogue is reproduced and can be seen as fiction.

Although the author and publisher have made every effort to ensure that the information in this book was correct at press time, the author and publisher do not assume and hereby disclaim any liability to any party for any loss, damage, or disruption caused by errors or omissions, whether such errors or omissions result from negligence, accident, or any other cause.

© 2020 Ella Marques, *Coming Home to Venus*

Graphics work Bianca Cutait

www.artefundamental.com.br

Proofreading and technical support by Hatch Editorial Services, www.hatch-books.com

Published by Coral Orchid Press, North Miami, FL

Printed in the USA

ISBN: 978-0-9987029-4-0 Paperback

ISBN: 978-0-9987029-5-7 E-Book

Visit us at: www.ellamarques.com

Coming Home to Venus

Contents

Coming Home to Venus

Introduction

In my first book, *I Was Born a Boy, from Venus*, I wrote my autobiography, stories about the great life experiences I had, about the struggles I went through, and about the beginnings of my transition. This book, *Coming Home to Venus*, is about my transition, from the first steps I took up to gender reassignment surgery, what happened, the changes I went through, the lessons I learned, the changes in and to my environment, the similar experiences of others, and what I expect for the future. Some fiction is included, and names have been changed. The book contains such themes as gender dysphoria, hormone replacement therapy (HRT), acceptance, procedures, gender reassignment surgery, and ID changes.

This book is not only a sort of guidance for transgender people who are transitioning but also a book for those who are not transgender, cis people. For them it's about understanding, acceptance, and compassion for us. (I have lived through some interesting experiences, so I also hope the book is entertaining!)

For both of my books, there are several reasons for me to write about the transgender theme. One of them is that I would like to share my extraordinary life with the people I know and love, my family and close friends. Another is that I would like to inform those people with whom I do not have much contact about my transition. Finally, I want to show all readers, whether they are transgender or not, an example of what transgender people go through to find themselves. It is not an option; it's the way we are born.

At this point, I would like to thank all my friends for being there for me, especially some special people who have a special place in my heart: my daughter, Victoria, and her great husband Tommy; my son David and his incredible wife, Gabby, who is the mother of my first grandchild; and my son Raphael and his girlfriend Julie. I would like to thank both of my ex-wives for the great times we had together. To my Portuguese family, in particular my sister, Luisa, I'm sorry I have not been there much lately. Last but not least, I would like to thank all the friends that have supported me for a short or a long time; there are many, many of them in the latest phase, mainly Missy, Bonnie, Bianca, Jessmarie, Jessica, just to mention a few. Another incredible set of people for whom I have a lot to thank are my counselors, Dr. Carol Clark, Lisa Shapiro, and all the others, as well as all of the doctors and their incredible staff that helped me so much, including Dr. Chettawut, Dr. Jason Cooper, and the late Dr. Greenwald.

Everything to be an Addict

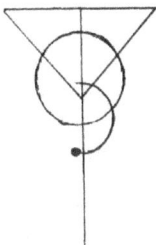

"We are addicted to our thoughts. We cannot change
anything if we cannot change our thinking."
— **Santosh Kalwar**,

Fernando opened the door of the large, white SUV
and said to his wife, "Thank you for the lift." He
walked to the back of the car as the door was power-
lifting, took his luggage out, pressed the down
button of the rear door, and said again, "I will call
you when I get to the hotel. Bye, love you."

His wife, Kate, told him, "Have a nice trip."

The white SUV started rolling away from Fort
Lauderdale-Hollywood International Airport's
Terminal 3, and Fernando walked to the check-in
area for US Airways. It was a beautiful Floridian day,
hot with a temperature hovering around eighty-six
degrees and low winter humidity. He printed out

his boarding card, and with it in hand, he walked over to the check-in counter.

"Going to Toronto?" asked the US Airways employee, a luggage tag in her hand.

"Yes, I am," answered Fernando, putting his luggage on the scales of the check-in counter.

"Please give me your boarding card and ID."

Fernando got out his wallet again, took out his ID, and handed it together with his boarding pass to the girl. "Here you have it," he said.

She checked all of the papers, put the tag on his luggage, and handed both documents to Fernando again. "Okay, you are good to go. Have a nice trip."

Fernando walked to the outside of the terminal. As soon as he was outside, he took a pack of Marlboro Lights and a lighter out of his carry-on. He started smoking as he walked to the smokers' corner of the airport.

'Another work trip, I hope it pays off. I need at least three machines this year to get by,' thought Fernando while having a deep inhale at his cigarette. There were other people in the smokers' corner, but he did not feel like talking to them. A very nice woman had just passed by, going in the direction of the airport, and Fernando was checking her out in detail, as usual. 'Well,' he thought, 'nice girl, wonderful makeup. I like the way the tight trousers show her very nicely shaped ass. Oh my God, I would love those boobs; they look so full and great. I just think the colors that she is wearing are too dark.' Fernando could not take his eyes off any girl; he was always looking at what they were wearing, the way they moved, how were they shaped. It was a real magnet.

The size and shape of boobs were always fascinating to him. It was total envy. Boobs, or *breastology*, as Fernando liked to call it, including bras, were a theme of obsession for him, but not in a sexual way. Fernando was fascinated by breasts and bras; even the passwords he used on his computer contained bra names and breast sizes.

After two quickly puffed cigarettes and some thoughts about the girl he was looking at, he headed back into the terminal and made his way through security.

He was then inside the terminal with another half hour until he had to board the plane, so he headed to the nearest bar. He checked for a nice, cozy seat with some space for his hand luggage and coat, and sat down.

"What would you like to drink?" asked the barman.

Coming Home to Venus

"Give me a glass of chardonnay," said Fernando.

"What about something to eat?"

"Nothing, thank you," answered Fernando.

As usual at midday, the bar was quite full. While waiting for his drink, Fernando got out his phone and started looking at emails, texts, and general notifications.

"Here's your drink, sir," said the barman, handing a glass of chardonnay to Fernando.

"So where are you going?" asked the man next to Fernando. He was a large, white man, with short, brown hair and a well-cut three-day beard.

"Toronto, to the cold, and you?" replied Fernando.

"I am going back home, west to Denver, Colorado," the man said and took a sip of a clear drink that looked like a gin and tonic.

"Oh, nice town. I've been there many times and love to go up to the Rockies and eat at the Fort, near Denver," answered Fernando while looking at his flight app to see if he had been upgraded. Well, bingo, he was going to be upgraded to first class on the way to Charlotte, North Carolina, his first stop.

After he boarded the plane where he was placed in first class, he spent the flight drinking white wine and playing Sudoku on his phone. It was a very normal flight.

"We are approaching Charlotte, North Carolina, and we will land in about thirty minutes. I hope you had a pleasant flight and thank you for flying US Airways," said the captain.

Fernando started to think. 'I have some time in this airport, so what shops am I going to visit? Brighton's—Manuela needs some nice rings—or maybe the shop on the corner of Terminal C and the atrium with the silver jewelry? There is Francesca's as well and the other shop in the corridor between the Atrium and Terminal D. I like this airport and I spend so much time here; it is the connection hub for many destinations in North America and it is quite modern.' This was just the start of the dream; he was dreaming of nice rings, earrings, bracelets, and turning the page to bras, panties, and dresses. This was a fixation he had not been able to stop since he was five years old. He had always identified as a woman, but he was brought up to be a man. It was expected of him to be masculine and show the world that he loved women and was the main breadwinner of his family. It was expected of him, and so he assumed the role. He had done so for a long time. He was fifty-eight years old and was still playing that role, the one that was expected by society.

I believe that some explanations are in order. For your understanding, Fernando is the name that the person we are writing about was born with, but Manuela was the name that Fernando identified with. He always knew that he was not a he but a she; that is where she found peace. In reality Fernando and Manuela were the same human being.

The flight finally landed and parked to the gate. Fernando got his hand luggage and walked off the plane, into Terminal B, through the atrium, and entered Brighton, a jewelry and fashion store, and started looking around. Immediately an elderly woman came up to him. "How can I help you? Buying a present for your wife? I am sure she would like one of our charm bracelets. What about the love theme?"

"Yes, why not. I think she would love it, and you know, her birthday is coming up," Fernando answered, knowing full well that the present was really for his female side, Manuela. The bracelets at Brighton's were just amazing, mainly because of the way their custom beads let a person tell their story. He was always looking for beads with a nautical theme—shells, sailing boats, representations of gorgeous mermaids with wonderful-looking breasts, just the ones he always dreamed of having.

After looking at the various pieces, he decided to buy a beautiful bracelet made of a kind of a gold knit with magnetic clasps, and some beads representing the sea and sailing boats. He loved it; it represented things he was really fond of, the sea and gold. He went to the counter and paid for it.

"Your wife will love it. Oh, you have such great taste," said the girl at the counter as she packed the bracelet in a very nice gift wrapping.

Fernando paid and said, "I am sure she will, believe me," and left the shop, walking to the middle of the atrium, where there was a sushi bar he he often went to on business trips.. He sat down and ordered a miso soup and a rainbow sushi roll. 'Soon I will be in my room, where I can be myself,' he thought as he ate.

The flight to Toronto was ready. Fernando boarded the plane and slept quite well waking up as they drew close to the beautiful Canadian city. The flight to Toronto over Lake Ontario is just fantastic, especially in winter when part of the lake is frozen. This time he was flying Air Canada, quite a nice airline, with good service and new planes. Toronto is a beautiful city, very impressive, and the night approach into the Mississauga airport is quite spectacular with all the lights of the city and some impressive landmarks such as the CN Tower on the horizon. The landing was perfect as it was most of the time, and Fernando was soon in Customs, showing his passport and entering Canada. It is really a wonderfully diverse country with a large number of ethnicities that somehow respect their ancestry more than the US or most other countries in North and South America do. Fernando would have moved there in a heartbeat if the winters weren't so cold.

Fernando got his luggage, smoked a cigarette outside of the airport, got his car at Avis, and drove to the hotel, a modern one next to his customer's place in Mississauga, not too far from the airport. He parked the car, had another cigarette on the way into the hotel, checked in, and went out for his final cigarette of the day in that bitter winter cold of Toronto before going up to the room.

Finally he was on his own, the transformation started as he opened the door to the room, and Manuela's evening routine immediately began. First he placed his traveling bag on the small ottoman and got out all the essential feminine things that always traveled with him: a bra, panties made of silk or a very feminine knit material, and a silk nightdress. He placed them all on top of the bed. Then he would undress as fast as he could, get into those fantastic clothes, and wow—Fernando was gone and Manuela was there, finally feeling as she was supposed to be. Going to bed, feeling her femininity, feeling herself, was a kind of wonderful cloud; she was not sure what type, a kinky one, a blue, pink, or even golden one. She got out of bed to get the bracelet that Fernando had bought earlier to put it on and dream again. The nightie was Manuela's evening routine; when she arrived early, she would have a dress, some sexy shoes, a wig, and very often even makeup. Most of the time she would stay in the room, enjoying her femininity; on rare occasions she would go out to anonymous places, though there was somehow a total fear of being discovered.

It was late, and Manuela fell asleep on this spun-sugar cloud of feelings, thinking how nice it was to be home. The problem with a dream, though, is that when you get up, the dream ends, and the next morning the feeling of guilt opened up to swallow her whole. Manuela ceased to exist and Fernando had to put on the show. Get up, take a shower, brush his teeth, shave, take the feminine vitamins, get dressed in the shitty male clothes, yes, the ones he was supposed to wear to work. Get breakfast, organize himself, get in the car, and drive to the customer. The feminine feeling had to stop there. 'What if the customer notices that I was wearing feminine clothes, or even worse, what if I start to act like a girl, showing emotions and talking girlishly?' he wondered.

The customer's factory was not far away, so it only took a couple of minutes to arrive there. Fernando got out of the car, got his briefcase—or traveling office, as he called it—walked to the main door, and entered the building. At reception he asked the girl behind the counter, "Could you tell John W. that Fernando is here?"

"Hi, can you please sign in?" answered the girl and then called John.

"Thank you. Wow, it is really cold here! You could freeze to death at this temperature," said Fernando.

"Yes, it is. We are used to it, though, and even like that we are freezing all the time," answered the receptionist.

"Yes, that is why there are so many Ontario people in Florida at this time of the year, escaping from the cold here. Snowbirds, I suppose," said Fernando.

"Yes, the privileged ones," she answered.

In the meantime John arrived.

"Hi Fernando, how was the trip? Hope you are keeping warm," said John.

"Doing great, my friend. Great trip, well, except for the cold here in Canada," answered Fernando. "How are you doing, sir? Is the business treating you okay?"

"I am doing great, but work has not really picked up yet. We expect that it will pick up later in the year, but we're not much spending right now."

"Yes, that seems to be a general trend. And how are our machines doing? Even if you do not have much to do?" asked Fernando.

"We are experiencing some issues with the taping machine. We talked to the factory in Switzerland, and they are looking at our software right now. There are too many stops. Anyway, let's go down to the shop floor to see what the girls can tell us," said John.

John took Fernando to a conference room, where they had an initial discussion about the new machine specifications and the alternatives that John had. Yes, the MI 303, the small machine, would be okay for his work. Afterward, they went to the factory where Fernando was received very well as usual. They discussed the machine stops, and he could see that the technical issues were caused by a defective sensor.

Fernando spent a good part of the day in the factory, with a small stop at a nearby sushi place for lunch. In the late afternoon, after the long meeting, he drove back to the hotel. He had his cigarette before going in, almost freezing his face off because of the cold. He went up to the room and took off his coat, jacket, pullover, shirt, and trousers as fast as he could. He then opened his luggage, took out a beautiful bra and put it on, followed by a dark-blue, knitted, roll-neck dress, which was good for the cold. There was no need to change into panties; Fernando had worn women's panties for many years underneath his male clothes. Kate knew about his tendencies since the day they had met, and she accepted it quite well, that is as long as it was not too obvious. Sometimes he would even wear a bra if he had a pullover on top. Then he took his socks off and put on some high-heeled shoes. He had about two hours before he would have dinner with the customer in a nice downtown restaurant. During that time he would be Manuela and work on the visit report, check and answer his emails, and make some calls to customers and business partners. Later that night he got dressed again as Fernando in all those uncomfortable clothes and conducted his business with his customer at a well-drunk and well-eaten dinner. When that ended, it was the same drill: coming to the hotel to change into Manuela, with her nightie and her girlie thoughts.

The next day there were two clients to visit—one in the morning, the other in the afternoon—followed by a flight to Montreal in the evening. It was another routine day of being Fernando with clients, and Manuela when alone.

Business was starting to grow, though insecurities abounded. There were many fears that customers had to overcome, but the future was going to be good and prosperous. At least Fernando thought this would be the case, but his feelings were somehow deteriorating. He had to have a lot of patience for his business as it developed, and in the time he had for himself, he felt that something was missing and he was not happy.

On the afternoon of the next day, he drove to the airport, left the car at Avis, entered the terminal, went directly to the men's restroom, got inside a cubicle, and put on a bra that was waiting in a very accessible part of his luggage. Then he went to the check-in area.

Wearing a bra for Fernando had quite a lot of meaning. The first was that it was a sign of femininity, so it made him feel more comfortable in his own skin; then when it was cold it was a way to keep his nipples from rubbing against the clothing. He had been taking natural hormones for a number of years, which affected his mood and made his nipples very soft and sensitive. The feeling of having estrogen in his body was a must; he could not get away from it. It just made him feel right. Too much testosterone made him depressive. But the drugs he was taking were over the counter and there was no prescription or follow-up with a specialist, so its effectiveness was probably not the best. The feeling of having estrogen gave him a kind of peace, though; somehow the feelings were right, not something he had to fight against.

"Montreal," said Fernando to the lovely attendant at the Air Canada check-in counter, handing her his passport.

The girl took the passport, looked at the screen, and said, "The flight is on time. Do you have any luggage?"

"Yes, one piece." He put his suitcase on the scale next to her. "Very nice earrings. Where did you get them? I should buy some for my wife."

"Oh, thank you. I bought them in downtown Toronto, but I am not sure of the name of the shop. I think it was something European."

"Oh, I'll have to check it out the next time I am in Toronto," Fernando said.

"Here," she said. "You have the boarding card and your luggage receipt. The flight is on time and I wish you a great trip."

Toronto to Montreal is a short flight, and very soon Fernando was in the hotel again, again near the airport. He checked in, went for a quick dinner at a sports bar, and then had his last cigarette and was back to the old routine: girlie clothes, read emails, make business reports, and finally, finally, go to different websites to check out women's clothes, makeup, YouTube makeup tutorials, and various sources of information for people like him. The internet had really changed a lot; the information was there, and it was easy to find. In the old days information about transgender people or transsexuals or transvestites came from sex shops or libraries. It was very difficult to find something unless you were part of the transgender community that existed in big cities like New York, London, and Los Angeles. Fernando remembered the days that he had gone out in New York with the girls, first as a man and later as a woman. There were special bars and restaurants for people just like him; by no means was he the only one.

The next day he had one customer meeting in the morning and then went back home to Fort Lauderdale, Florida. As Fernando arrived at the airport in the late afternoon, his wife picked him up and drove him home, where he cooked for the whole family and they all sat at the table in front of the television.

"How was your trip, Papi?" asked Victoria, his youngest daughter.

"Quite good, we should get an order for one of the companies in Toronto I visited in the last week. But it was so cold, something like minus-ten degrees Celsius. It was so cold that sometimes I could not even finish my cigarette outside; otherwise my nose would freeze."

"Well, you know you should stop smoking. It's no good for you," continued Victoria.

Fernando poured another glass of chardonnay, and when he finished eating he went to the garden, where he sat and did his home routine, meaning that he stayed outside until late at night smoking, drinking, playing computer poker, solitaire, or looking at websites about girls' clothes, crossdressers, and transgender people. This was his life at home. There were no girlie clothes, but there was smoke, alcohol, and video games. The routine was starting to take over his life, and he felt more and more miserable every minute of it. On the weekends, instead of wine, Fernando would drink whisky, and sometimes he would just simply fall asleep. He would not tell anybody about his feelings; he was getting more and more bottled up and depressed, taking it all out with alcohol, cigarettes, and games. Real addictions. During the day he would work as much as he could; he was a real workaholic, but he did not have many interactions with friends, or even with his family.

At home there were no girlie clothes, just panties and bras underneath his male clothes. At night he would wear a nice, female nightgown. It had been many years since the last time he wore male PJs, and Kate was ok with it. When the family was out, he would go full girlie, wearing nice dresses and skirts, putting on makeup, and wearing wigs. He was finally himself—that is, until they came back and misery came back with them.

Fernando was also taking so-called "natural estrogens," plant-based, over-the-counter medicine that had a high estrogen content. He had been taking this kind of medicine for at least fourteen years, sometimes at a higher dosage and sometimes at a lower one without medical support or prescriptions. These medicines had a very strong influence on his mood and on his body's shape. Sometimes he even got scared because suddenly his nipples would get very sensitive and small drops of lactation would come out. When he got scared, he would reduce the dosage and hope that all would be better. These were the typical influences of HRT, but he had no real control over it because it was "homemade," without looking at hormone levels or blood tests.

Coming Home to Venus

I Knew I Had Gender Dysphoria

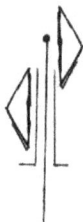

"It's easy to fictionalize an issue when you're not aware of the many ways in which you are privileged by it."
— **Kate Bornstein, <u>Gender Outlaws: The Next Generation</u>**

Well, depression was at home. One-night Fernando got drunk and played so much poker that the next morning he felt really bad. His head was spinning, he was feeling lonely and lost, and his guilt went through the roof; he could not see himself anymore. He had to do something about it, get some help, and I mean professional help. That night he thought to himself, 'I cannot live like this anymore. I am losing all control. My nerves are getting out of hand. I have to do something about it. Tomorrow I will look for help.'

The next step was finding a counselor that could help him, someone who knew about addictions, about sex, and about transgender issues. It did not take long to find someone on the internet called Dr. Carol Clark.[i] She knew a great deal about all the issues for which Fernando was seeking answers.

The next steps were quite simple: to contact Dr. Clark and make an appointment. Fernando got a lot of homework right off the bat, a large questionnaire that he answered the best way possible and in great depth. Finally the day came that he was going to have his first counseling hour. At this point, I would like to state that counseling and what is discussed in support groups is confidential information, so what I am writing here should be considered fiction and anonymous, but is based on factual experiences. I would like to add as well that many of the experiences that transgender people experience, are very similar, so they describe general experiences of transgender people.

It was a Thursday morning as Fernando drove down to Miami, to the house and office of Dr. Clark. She always made sure that her patients had a high level of confidentiality, so he had to wait outside until the car of the appointment before him pulled out of its parking place. He parked and rang the doorbell and waited, looking at a massive, magnificent tree in the driveway.

Coming Home to Venus

It did not take long for the door to open and a very nice-looking, slim lady with dark brown hair and a friendly smile appeared. "You must be Fernando, she said. "Hi, please come in and sit down."

"Yes, Dr. Clark, nice to meet you," Fernando said and entered the house, and then the room where all of their talk would take place.

"Sit down, make yourself comfortable. Would you like tea? Or some water?" asked Dr. Clark as Fernando sat down in a comfortable, upholstered armchair.

"Water would be great," he said. "Nice to meet you. I read your profile online, and I think I am speaking with someone who can understand me. Did you get the file I sent you with the answers to your questions?"

"Yes, I received them, but why don't you tell me about yourself, your feelings, and why are you here," said Dr. Clark as she got a cup and filled it with cold water and handed it to Fernando.

"Well, where shall I start?" he said. "I am fifty-eight years old. I was born in Portugal and have two nationalities, Portuguese and Swiss. I have lived in many countries, traveled a lot, and have been living in the United States for four years now. I am in my second marriage; I have three children, and the youngest is living here in the US with me and my wife. I came here today because I am depressed. I have not told any of my intimate feelings to anybody for a long time, and this is eating me up. I have been drinking a lot lately, I smoke almost two packs of cigarettes a day, I play all sorts of electronic games, and I always have the same thoughts about my identity. I want to wear women's clothes all the time. I want to do female things, and this is forbidden to me."

"What is forbidden? Wearing women's clothes? Who is denying you this?" said Dr. Clark.

"Well, society is denying me this," he started. "I am married, I am a businessperson, and people expect me to act according to their standards. But I always have worn women's clothes since I was very young, ever since I can remember.

"About twenty-five years ago I visited a counselor in Switzerland, and I started to accept myself, started to have other friends that had the same inclination as I do, and life started to become more self-assured. In the beginning I called myself Florence, and later Manuela, because it was easy to get a credit card with that name since my second name is Manuel. Then my psychologist sent me to the university hospital in Zurich to see a psychiatrist. Yes, it was time to go one step further and start

HRT. I had about six months of regular meetings with a student doctor and told them all of my story. Then I finally met the doctor, and it was a real disaster. He told me that I was a gay guy and that the only thing I had in mind was cocks and I didn't need any hormones.

"My self-confidence just fell like a heavy stone. I could not identify myself with the image he portrayed of me. I told him so and he showed his disagreement. As I left the therapy I felt dirty and terrible. I was shaking and only had one thing in my mind: to commit suicide. It took me a couple of days and a large amount of alcohol to get back on my feet, and then by extreme coincidence I met a girl that became later my second wife.

"Yes, it brought my thoughts to another level, and I started to feel good again. I dumped all of my female clothes and thought, 'This time is for real; I will not have to wear those clothes anymore.' I even was clean for a couple of months, and then, there we go again, I started to buy panties and bras and all the rest. Then I started to look for hormones and found some natural ones on the internet, which I am still taking. Since then I have been dressing as a woman in my closet. I don't go out, I gained about sixty pounds, and am quite addicted to cigarettes and my work. I have quite a good career and decent jobs, always traveling. I should stop doing this, but I don't know what to do anymore. I feel so guilty."

Fernando wasn't sure what Dr. Clark would make of his monologue, so he looked up at her cautiously, hoping she would understand more than the Swiss psychiatrist had.

"Okay," Dr. Clark said, thinking over everything she had heard. "Have you ever thought about trusting and understanding your feelings? It looks like the main issue is that on one side you have some very persistent and deep feelings and on the other, somewhere in your brain, there is a command that tells that you are not allowed to have them. This gap creates in you an obvious depression and frustration, leading you to be addicted. And I don't mean in the regular sense of alcohol or drug abuse, but addition to games, tobacco, work, and all the other things. You should read my book *Addict America*,"[ii] she said. "I see where your problem lies. I am having a transgender support group meeting tomorrow at seven o'clock in Wilton Manors. Can you come?"

"What is it all about? What do I have to do?" asked Fernando.

"Well, it's a group of people like you that come together on a regular basis and discuss their issues, their experiences, frustrations, and achievements. We have a meeting every month. They are all transgender people there, transgender families and therapists. The meeting is one and a half hours long, and it is free of charge, just a small voluntary donation for the room. You don't have to come but it would be really good for you to see that you are not alone, that there are many people like you and that you all have very similar lives and issues and learn to understand yourself through the various experiences." said Dr. Clark.

For the rest of the meeting Fernando talked about his feelings, experiences, his addiction, thoughts, and mainly about his different steps in life. It is quite a relief to talk about issues that are so deeply rooted and one learns such a lot just by listening to oneself, sometimes some of these issues were so packed that there was a difficulty to even recognize them. Dr. Clark reminded him of the meeting before he left, where and when it was taking place.

The therapy session finally ended, and he drove home, then went to his usual place in the garden with a cigarette in his hands. He took a deep breath and thought, 'Oh my god, what have I done? I am so excited, like a new life is starting, but where is it going? What will happen to me? Is it going to be a positive step in my life? I am scared and anxious, but I'm also happy. What is going on?' That night his mind could not switch off and he was starting to dream about dancing in a beautiful chiffon dress, so light and stunning, showing the femininity of the person wearing it.

Fernando told his wife Karen that he was going to see a therapist, and that he was going to the support group, something that she welcome, accepted and understood. He invited her to participate in these support groups as well, and later in the transitions she did attend some as well.

The next day came, and his heart was beating with high expectations and strong fears. Around six he started to drive to Wilton Manors, taking the North Federal Highway, that is a very important north south road in Florida. There was the usual Friday evening traffic, but he arrived about five minutes before the start of the meeting. Some people were sitting or else positioning chairs in a circle. Dr. Clark was helping set up some of the chairs, so he approached her and said, "Hi, Dr. Clark."

She answered, "Hi, Manuela, welcome to the group." The chairs were in a circular position, and most of the people were sitting.

He started to look at the people that were sitting and the ones that were coming in. Some appeared to be cis women, some were clearly transgender woman, and one was a transgender man. Many of the trans women were not very passable while some others looked passable and beautiful. There were also some male-seeming people dressed in men's clothes, Fernando included, and he was sitting next to Dr. Clark. Everybody was talking with each other; there were some clear friendships in the group. Some people were still coming in, some were late. Seven o'clock had already come and gone, and there were about thirty-five people in the room.

"Ladies and gentlemen, let's start this meeting," Dr. Clark said in a loud voice. Most of the crowd stopped their conversations to listen to her. "As we get started, let me remind you of the rules, please respect each other, don't interrupt each other, and most important of all, what is told here stays here and will not be shared outside. This is a safe zone for you, so please respect it. As usual we will start by going around, and each person will present himself or herself with their name, age, preferred pronouns, and whatever else you have in your heart, like your recent experiences. We will then discuss any topics you want. You can start, Ellen."

The woman who stood was obviously an elderly lady, with a strong, masculine look because of her big belly and lack of feminine posture. She sounded like a very nice person but still was in the process of changing. "My name is Ellen," she said. "I am one thousand years old in transgender years. I am a male-to-female or MTF transgender person, and I am very surprised and confused about the names that we are popping out all of a sudden for the LGBT community, and I would like to talk to you all about this."

After Ellen the crowd presented themselves one by one. Some were cis women and men presenting as such; they were mainly counselors or students of Dr. Clark. Some were female-to-male (FTM) trans people, and others were MTF, all ranging in age from their twenties to their seventies. Most MTFs were dressed as women, except Fernando and another person; most FTMs had on trousers and a T-shirt. One was a very passable men; the others looked more androgynous. It then came time for Fernando to present himself.

"Hi, my name is Fernando—that is, Manuela. This is the first time I have attended such a group. I believe I am a MTF transgender woman. Thank you for having me here," he said.

The discussions started, and Ellen introduced the first big theme. "I have been in transition for over fifteen years, and right now there is a big flow of new names that I don't understand anymore. First, we were called transvestites, crossdressers, drag queens, or drag kings, and some names were for people that were not living full time in their preferred gender. Then came the name transsexual, whatever that meant, because we are changing our gender and not all of us change our sexual orientation. Well, for many years we got used to the term transsexual. Then there were a lot of very pejorative names for transgender women that started to come mostly from the porn industry such as trans, tranny, or she-male or ladyboy. We started to understand those names and what it meant, and the term transgender is a quite recent one, probably not older than ten years. But now there is a new wave of names coming such as genderfluid, nonbinary, that refer to people that can identify with one or the other gender, depending on the day or on whatever is happening. Does anybody have knowledge of these names and fully understand them?"

"Yes, Ellen, I think you are right. For someone outside, it's very confusing and some of these names are actually meant to be very pejorative and not nice at all to the community. I would propose that someone would get the full list together, adding what is acceptable or not, and share it," said Dr. Clark. "I mean, tranny and ladyboy are very judgmental names that we do not and will not accept here."

The meeting went on. As usual the one and a half hours of the meeting were not long. Most people talked but some came up short, either because of time or because they were afraid to share.

For Fernando It was the first time he had been in such a meeting and the only time that he dressed as a man at one.

Driving home, he was thinking, "Oh my god, there are so many people like me that have the same feelings and share similar experiences. Is it really possible for me to transition and live as a woman? Am I really a woman or just some kind of pervert? My mother always told me that I am a man. She never accepted my feminine attitude—as a matter of fact, she always punished me for it."

That night Fernando did not sleep. He spent the night in bed mainly thinking about two things: his feelings about what was going on with him and why he had such feelings in the first place. They had been there for such a lot of time, and they refused to disappear. He had done all possible to forget, but they just came back again and again. The second thing he was thinking about was what were the logistics in getting out of the house a boy, arriving at the next meeting as a girl, and coming back home as a boy, all without being spotted or having issues.

The weeks that followed were probably some of the most important in Fernando's life. He frequently thought about himself, his feelings, and where he wanted to be and what he wanted to do in life. He thought of the year before when he had been sailing in Norway with some friends and his depression started to kick in.

At that time one of his good friends told him, "You're a businessperson. How many business plans have you created for the companies you worked for?"

"I cannot count anymore," said Fernando. "I did so many of them for my previous company and when I was a consultant."

"Have you ever tried to do one for your own life?" his friend asked. "Putting together your strengths, weaknesses, opportunities, and threats; trying to dig into your history and biography; thinking about where you want to go and how can you do this? You know, set up your goals."

"Wow, you are so right," Fernando had said. "I think it's really logical, what you do for others you can certainly do for yourself."

When he had come back to Florida, he started to write his business plan and as he had done before he started by telling his own story. Then he came across a major issue: Who the hell was he? He had been functioning all his life, but was that living? His feelings had been manipulated from a tender age, and he had forgotten all about that. Yes, all his life he had tried to forget his feelings; he was trying to be nice to others and forget himself, just function.

So, when he started to talk to Dr. Clark about those real feelings, the thing he had forgotten or hidden all his life, he had a head start, one year of dwelling on these feelings and experiences. With the professional help of this wonderful person, those feelings just rolled out faster. She used a number of techniques that proved to be very effective, and the mental blockades started to be removed. All of sudden he was remembering his youth, he was trusting and following his feelings, and Fernando was slowly gone, giving place to Manuela, who would later become me, Ella. The whole process did not take more than six months of intensive follow-up.

The support group was a monthly meeting, and I could not wait until I could come out as Manuela. There was a lot of work, like getting the right clothes. Since Fernando thought that he was not allowed to shop at stores for women's clothes, he got them from the internet, from Amazon, from crossdresser supply stores. Then there was the makeup, which I tried until I got it right—thank God for YouTube tutorials. I can assure you that I was totally alone. Nobody would help me; even my partner at the time, Karen, who was fully aware of everything was understanding but, unsupportive as far as my clothes were concerned.

Finally, the day came. I had made a little bag with all my girlie things in it. I was wearing the lacy underwear as usual, and left home in the big car. Near the meeting venue, I found an industrial building with nobody in the parking lot stopped the car there and changed over. Fernando was starting to become Manuela. It was not easy to change, though, because the car did not have much space and there was not much light for makeup. My makeup mirror was the rearview mirror of the car, which was definitely not ideal. I was running late and taking longer than I had expected, so I had to go. I drove to the meeting place, got out of the car, arranged my skirt and slowly went in. I was probably not the best-looking girl. I had a big belly at the time, not the most ladylike manners, and terrible makeup, but in such meetings, there was no discrimination and no mutual criticism. We were all learning. Some were fully realized women and men, and some of us were taking baby steps.

I as Manuela entered the meeting room, obviously with little or no self-confidence. By God was I nervous, and you could say my legs were kind of shaking.

I was immediately greeted with comments from Dr. Clark. "Well, look who is here! Manuela, I think I want to see you like this all the time."

"Thank you, Dr. Clark. I think I have a lot to learn still," I said.

"No worries. all goes step by step, you will see. "

The group started as usual with the introductions. This time I said, "My name is Manuela, and I am an MTF transgender woman!" I was starting to understand who I really was.

During the meeting there was a lot of discussion about all of our pasts and what we had in common in our past lives.

"When I was young, I could not understand that I couldn't live as a girl," said Maribel, who would become one of my very good friends. "Coming from a Latino family, the thought of a transgender kid was not possible. Well, most people did not even know what that was.

"So as my puberty came, I started to be rebellious and criticize everything. My parents didn't know what to do with me, it was just too complicated, so they decided to subcontract my education and send me to boarding school. They sent me for three years to a lovely place in Spain. I was still very rebellious and was punished for it a lot, but it opened my eyes a lot. As far as my femininity is concerned, it got the short straw. I could not dress up; it was very difficult."

"Wow, what a coincidence," I said. "I had the same experience. My parents gave me the choice of a Jesuit school, or a school in Switzerland. The thought of going to a school full of priests was the last thing I wanted, so I chose the school in Switzerland. I had a great time there, had lots of friends; some of them are still my best friends. As far as femininity is concerned, well, there was the big blocker. I had no time for it, just like you, Maribel."

Maribel, like many transgender women, told her very interesting story, and it made me think of one remarkable thing that is so common among transgender women. During their teens many transgender women compensate with extreme male role plays. Some will join the police, the military, or do extreme sports. Maribel was a police officer for a while, doing crazy, dangerous work. Some famous transgender women like Caitlyn Jenner were very successful athletes in their past lives.

After some months of support groups and intense work with Dr. Clark, the common denominator of feeling was that all my life a woman was there inside me. Yes, I had played a role to try to show everyone that I was a man. Sometimes it was not very convincing, as I learned later, but it was mixed up with a very strong sense of nervousness and depression. Yes, I tried to please my mother who told me that I had to be a boy all my life. I had tried to commit suicide some three or four times, and now, there was a way to become free and see that true light, to be myself.

During this period there was a lot to learn about womanhood. All the things that most cis women learn from a tender age I had to learn as well: how to behave, for example; how to sit with a skirt the correct way, not showing my private parts; how to present in a feminine way, the moves, the gestures, and the ever-important walk. I wanted to have a normal feminine walk, not exaggerated and like a drag queen. I suppose many cis women are not good at this either, but at least they have some degree of learning. At the age of fifty-nine to relearn all of this was not easy, but it was possible. The idea of

Manuela was to be passable; she would go somewhere and people would take her as a woman and not as some kind of bird of paradise. The same went for my clothes and style. Everybody is somehow making a statement in life, and I had to find my presentation statement with nobody to help me.

The learning was also about treatments, about my body, about possible risks, and where I wanted to go and what I wanted to do in my life. One of the things that became clear to me was that hormones and surgery were not smoke friendly, so I had to do something about my cigarette habit before starting HRT.

Many great changes and ideas come during the night while people are sleeping, and Manuela for sure was no exception. One night I was in bed in a kind of thinking mode, something I do regularly, and my brain was saying, 'I will most probably start hormone replacement therapy very soon, but the risk of HRT and smoking is high. No doctor will give me a treatment if I do not stop immediately. And of course, why should I take that risk? It is time to stop and start to live healthier, and I mean now. Starting now, no more cigarettes, cigars, or whatever type of shit I can inhale."

Coming Home to Venus

I had my mind set. The next morning when I woke up, the first thing I did was to put away the cigarettes. I put them on the top shelf of a cupboard that was difficult to access. My first day without a smoke, my head was kind of spinning, but well, I survived and was proud of it. The second and third day as well—as a matter of fact the whole week— my head and body were getting very slowly back to normal. Of course, there were many moments where I questioned it all; all the time I thought, 'Is this the price I have to pay for my womanhood?' and the answer was always a big, fat *yes*.

Well, the result of giving up smoking was that I gained weight. My belly was growing, and my weight was going through the roof. I was feeling less and less attractive, and there was a strong connection for me between womanhood and attractiveness. So, it was time to go to a specialist and take the necessary steps to lose weight.

One day I got full of courage. I took the phone and dialed the number of a weight loss center near my house. "Hi, my name is Fernando. I want to lose weight, but I need help because I gave up smoking and my weight is going up like hell."

"Hi, my name is Pam. I am a nutritionist. You are in the right place. We are specialists in weight loss. You should come and see us. We weigh you on our special scales and find out more about your ideal weight and fat content, then we make you a diet accordingly so that you can have fast results. So when would you like to come?"

"Well, as soon as possible, when you have time," I said.

"Okay, what about tomorrow morning at ten o'clock?"

"That should be okay. I will come then. Tell me, how much will it cost?"

"Well, it depends on the treatment we will have for you. We can only know after examining you," said Pam.

The next day I went to the weight loss center. I presented as Fernando in men's clothes. It was a very clean and nice place, which almost looked like a doctor's office with small examining rooms.

At the counter there was a very pretty girl, who was quite slim and tidy-looking. I went over to her and said, "My name is Fernando. Could I talk to Pam?"

"Sure! I am Pam. You phoned yesterday, correct?"

"Yes, I did. Nice to meet you."

"I am just finishing up with a client. Please take a seat. I will be with you in five minutes." I sat down and looked at all the photos and promotional materials. There were "before and after" photos of people celebrating facts like, "I lost 58 pounds in just 5 months!" or, "I lost over 100 pounds in just over one year." It all seemed very promising.

"So now I have time for you. Please come with me," said Pam, and she walked up the corridor and into a white room with a brown desk, comfortable armchairs, and of course the scale that we expected. "Please sit down and let's talk."

"Okay," I said. "I want to lose weight. I see that you are the experts, so let me know what to do, how much it costs, and well, all the information."

"Sure. So, we are a weight loss center, we can help you lose weight." She gave a complete speech about the center, its methods, B12 shots and hormone shots. At the end she said, "First let's see how tall you are," and pointed to the wall where there was a measuring tape and a wedge. I positioned myself against the wall for the measurement. "Five feet six," Pam said. "Is this correct?"

I answered, "It looks like I am shrinking. I used to be five seven."

"Now please step up to the scales and take off your shoes."

I took off my shoes and stepped up to the scales. Pam manipulated the machine, and all of a sudden there was a small piece of paper coming out with a lot of data.

"Okay, we are done," said Pam. "You can sit."

I stepped down, and Pam took the piece of paper. We both sat, and Pam started analyzing the data.

"Yes," she said,"you are obese. Your BMI is quite high, and there is quite a lot to do. You weigh 205 pounds. For your height and for being a man, you should be below 160 pounds, preferably 155. In other words you should lose at least 45 to 50 pounds."

"Wow! Oh my, that is a lot. What do I have to do to do that?"

"Well, we propose that you take some hormonal shots to help with your metabolism and some B12 shots, together with a special diet," said Pam.

"What kind of hormones are you talking about?" I asked.

Pam explained in detail the hormones in question and what was expected from them.

"Well, there is something you should know," I said. "I am transgender and I will start hormone replacement therapy quite soon. The main hormones that I will take will be estrogen. Do you think that there will be any conflict between the two types of hormones?"

Pam's mouth opened wide, and I could see the apparent shock on her face. She got herself together quickly and said, "I have no idea. I have to ask our doctor and will let you know. I will phone you, and then we will see what the next steps will be."

I left the office, after leaving all the necessary information. A day or so later, Pam phoned to tell me that the doctor left some information and that we should get together to discuss it, so I went to see Pam again.

"Well, darling, our doctor does not think that there will be interference between your HRT and our hormones, especially not in the first phase. So, do you want to go ahead with us?" asked Pam.

"Yes, I do. I really have to lose weight," I said.

"Okay, the first part of the diet is going to be a detox, so here is a flyer with all the details." She then explained the paper and all the details of the diet. "...and don't forget: no salt."

I paid and got my first weight-loss hormone injection. It was the beginning of a very interesting time. The results were quite amazing, as you will see.

In the meantime, the other battle of becoming more feminine was going on. I had more than six months of treatment and gender counseling. During this period, I came to terms with my real feelings. The shame was slowly vanishing; I could talk about those feelings without hiding them; I even went to a great effort to try to remember my youth in detail.

My feminine feelings had been there since the age of five. In the early sixties there was not much understanding of transgender people, and of course I was regularly punished for wearing girl's clothes. I remembered many special scenes such as one time when I was about five years old. I was in bed wearing a bra and some panties of her older sisters' underneath my PJs. This was something I did almost on a daily basis. This time it was in the morning and I was awake but still in a kind of daydreaming phase.

All of a sudden, my nanny opened the door and came in the room. She said, "Time to wake up, little boy. Come on out of bed. You have to go to kindergarten." As she said that she took the sheets off the bed and noticed that I was wearing a bra. "Fernando, what are you doing! You have girls' clothes on. I am going to call your mother."

"No, no, please don't tell her anything! She is going to punish me, you know that," I said, almost crying.

"Yes, you need to be punished to learn that boys don't wear girls' clothes. You are a boy, not a girl," said my nanny.

"No, no, no! I am a girl, I know that I am a girl. How do you know that I am a boy? I tell you I am a girl!" I said.

"Well, boy, what you have between your legs is something that only boys have. That is the only truth," said Nanny, and she ran out of the door to get my mother.

It did not take long for my mother to come, still in a morning gown. As she entered the room with my nanny, she looked at me and said, "Fernando, again? How many times did I tell you that boys don't wear girls' clothes? And on top of that the nice things I just bought your sisters! You have to take that out of your head. Men that do these things get killed or go to prison. Please stop immediately. So that you don't forget, I will give you a punishment on your bum. It will hurt and you will remember it for life."

She forced me to lie across her legs with my bum up, and with her heavy hands she hit me on my back side at least twenty times. It hurt, and I was crying. This was just an example of the many instances where I was punished for wearing girls' clothes and playing with my sisters' dolls.

Other more recent memories were coming from the time some twenty-five years before when I tried to transition for the first time. I was living in Switzerland then, divorced and living alone. It was an incredible time of change.

I had left my ex-wife to live alone in a big apartment. It was 1991, the internet was just starting out, and with it some information about what were called at the time travesties. As I was alone in the house, I immediately started to buy women's clothes from the catalogs and wear them after work. I was very fat then, too, so I started to lose weight—well, too much weight—and soon I got anorexia and weighed less than 130 pounds. I started to look feminine, well, androgynous and almost feminine.

One day I got my courage together and went to a crossdressers private gathering in Basel, at a club I had found online. The gathering was in a restaurant, and a lot of very well-dressed and presentable girls got together, talked, ate, and drank.

"Hi, what is your name?" one of them asked me. I was wearing a blouse and skirt and some not-so-well-done makeup and a terrible, cheap wig. At the time we all went to those meetings, and there was a changing room where all the girls would dress up and get prepared for the evening.

"Hi, my name is Florence," I answered Fernando, obviously shaking like a tree in the wind.

"Is this your first time here?"

"Yes, the first time, and I am so nervous," I answered.

"Don't worry, girl. We do not discriminate here, and believe me, all of us started like you the first time," said Nadine, one of the organizers. "Next week we are getting makeup training with some of the specialists from Globus. I am sure you will want to come as well. I will send you all the information."

All the girls sat in the restaurant and were talking about their lives, their friends and their feelings. I was not talking much, but observing, and somehow, I started to feel good and at home.

This part of my life could be another book. There is so much to tell about how I started to live and bloom as a woman. I would go out shopping in my woman self, and I got a credit card under the name of Manuela. During the day I passed as Fernando and was sales manager of a company with about ten people working for me. One day I was out in Oerlikon, shopping as usual, and all of a sudden one of my coworkers was next to me. I was paralyzed, and luckily my voice was as well. The person in question never recognized me, but I got really scared of being found out.

I thought, 'This is too dangerous. I will lose my job if I get caught; let's stop this." Once again, I started to throw away the dresses and underwear. I felt miserable. "Okay, next step, get help."

I looked for a psychologist in Basel and started to see her.

In the first meeting, Fernando was sitting in front of the psychologist as she asked, "So what brings you here? How can I help you?"

"Hi, it is not easy to tell you, how can I say? Well, I have this incredible urge all the time to wear women's clothes. I know it is really stupid, I don't know why I know this, I am really ashamed. By the way I am not gay," I answered with a high degree of embarrassment. "I want this to stop; I cannot have this all the time. I will lose my job if people know about it. Please help me stop this urge."

"If I understand correctly you cross-dress regularly in women's clothes. So what's wrong with that? You are not the only one. How do you feel when you have them on? Can you tell me?" asked the psychologist.

"Oh, I feel great! I feel peaceful, but the other day I was next to someone I know. Luckily he did not recognize me, but then I felt really ashamed and bad. I don't want to feel like that anymore," I said.

"Okay, there is nothing to be ashamed of, but let's see what is behind all this. Let's have some more sessions," said the psychologist.

I went to her regularly, first presenting as a man and then finally as a woman, when about one year later my psychologist told me, "Manuela, I cannot do anything for you anymore. For your development, you should start hormones, and I cannot prescribe this, so I will send a letter to the university hospital in Zurich where you can have a psychiatrist taking care of you."

This ultimately led to the head psychiatrist telling me I was a gay man and that he would not prescribe me hormones. This led me into a spiral of depression and suicidal thoughts.

All these thoughts and feelings came through my mind during my months of continuous counseling with Dr. Carol Clark. One day I arrived to my appointment and came out of the car, wearing a nice skirt and top. I was starting to feel much better. I sat in the comfortable seat in the consulting room, and started to talk.

"Hi, Dr. Clark. How are you doing? Look, I already lost about fifteen pounds since I started my diet," I said.

"Yes, I can see that. You are starting to look quite cute," said Dr. Clark. "I have a question for you. We have been having these sessions for quite a few months, and I will give you your letter if you want to start hormone replacement therapy. Do you already have an endocrinologist? Do you need me to refer someone?"

"Yes, I plan to ask my doctor if he can recommend someone," I said.

"Okay, as soon as you have an endocrinologist to take care of you, I will write you a letter with the confirmation that you have gender dysphoria and you can start HRT," said Dr. Clark.

Well, what I had been waiting for such a long time was finally there. I had been officially diagnosed with gender dysphoria,[iii] the basis to start my transition.

Since then, apparently some researchers have claimed that they can recognize transgender people by looking at a brain scan. We will see how this progresses.

Coming Home to Venus

The Magic of HRT

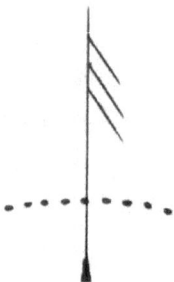

"Hormone blockers changed and saved my life."

Jazz Jennings

It was time to change, to start the transition. I was diagnosed with gender dysphoria, meaning I was experiencing distress as a result of the fact that the gender assigned at birth did not match my gender identity. Officially I was a transgender person. The next step would be to adjust my body to fit my gender Identity, starting with hormone replacement therapy (HRT).[iv]

The first step was to find an endocrinologist. I made an appointment with my regular practitioner in Boca Raton, a normal doctor for normal people without transgender experience nor understanding. I went to the doctor's office, and after the usual waiting time, they brought me to the examination room.

After a short time, the doctor came in and said, "Hi, Fernando, what brings you here?"

I was very nervous. I had to tell this person what I wanted, and that meant explaining that I was transgender. "I came here because I need a referral for an endocrinologist." The doctor looked at me with a very inquisitive face, so I carried on. "I have been diagnosed with gender dysphoria by my psychologist. I am transgender, and I want to start HRT."

"Okay, how long have you been experiencing this?" asked the doctor.

"Well, I have known about my feelings since I was about five years old. I have been in therapy with Dr. Carol Clark for almost six months now."

"We do not have much experience with this, but I will see what I can do. Stop by tomorrow and ask customer service for your referral. I will have to talk to the doctor first." Well. What a way to find out that the person who was with me was an assistant and not the doctor.

The next morning I went to the doctor's office and said, "Hi, my name is Fernando. I asked yesterday for a referral for an endocrinologist, and the doctor told me I should come here today to get it. Can you have a look?"

"Okay, let me check with the office manager," said one of the nurses, and she left to talk to her office manager. After some four or five minutes, she returned. "We don't have any information about your referral, but let me ask the doctor. Please take a seat, I will call you."

"Okay, I will wait," I said, and I went back to the waiting room.

After some fifteen minutes one of the office girls called, "Fernando, please come to the counter." When I did so, the girl there told me, "We do not have any records about your question, so a doctor will see you. Please come around back."

I was led to the doctor's office where I was told to sit and wait. About another ten minutes passed, and another doctor appeared, this time a young girl, not the same assistant as the previous day.

She came in and said, "My colleague did not say anything, so we have no record. Can you tell me why you are here?"

I repeated to her what I had told the woman at the front desk.

"Okay, can we see the letter?" said the girl.

"My counselor will write the letter to the name of the endocrinologist. I will bring you a copy as soon as I know who this person will be."

"Okay, I will talk to the doctor and will let you know tomorrow. Just phone the office to see if it is ready then."

I was getting frustrated, but I did not see any other alternative than to do what was expected of me. I went back home and started to research transgender-friendly doctors. As a matter of fact, there were not many specialists around my area, just a handful of them.

The next morning I picked up the phone and called the doctor's office. When someone picked up, I said, "Hi, my name is Fernando. I was with one of the doctor's assistants yesterday concerning a referral to an endocrinologist. Can I come pick up the referral?"

"Hi, Fernando, just give me a moment. I will transfer you our office manager," said the girl on the other end of the line.

Approximately two minutes later I was transferred to the office manager.

"Hi, Fernando. How are you?" she said. "We discussed your case with the doctor and his assistants, and I am sorry to tell you but we cannot refer you to any further specialists."

"Sorry," I said. "Why is that?"

There was a large silence on the other end of the line, and then there was a statement. "We don't deal with such things, thank you. Do you have any other questions?"

"I can't believe this! You are refusing to refer me because I am transgender? Thank you very much," I said and hung up. I felt horrible, discriminated or even violated of my rights as a person. I could not understand that a health specialist could be so terrible and refuse treatment to its patients. What could I do? Take them to court? I later understood through friends that this is just very common, some of us were even told, "Just leave my office."

I was determined to start HRT, so if my regular doctor would not do it, then the only real option was to change doctors, to find someone that specialized in transgender patients. The combined efforts of the internet and my friends produced some interesting results; there were about five places in my area that were transgender friendly. The next step was to find out if my insurance would accept these places. I finally got the address of an endocrinology care center that was transgender friendly. I made an appointment with Dr. Willy, gave the name and address to Dr. Clark, and she finally wrote the letter with the confirmation of gender dysphoria.

I had to wait two weeks until I saw Dr. Willy. That was really a very long time; on top of this I in had guests from Switzerland. All of this made me very nervous, especially since there was no room for my femininity and my natural expression.

Finally the day came. I dropped my friends off at a mall to go shopping, and I drove to the care center dressed as a man. I had no opportunity to do anything else. After I had been weighed and measured, I was brought to a small exam room. The temperature was set to very low, but the room looked like a hospital full of technical equipment. I sat down and waited for a few minutes.

"Hi, Fernando, how are you?" said a very nice African American woman. "I have some questions for you."

That was the beginning of a very long questionnaire. The nurse asked me my birth date to crosscheck the records; then she measured my blood pressure and started a very long questionnaire concerning my level of distress and my sexual orientation. She asked me about HIV, about my general health, the medicines I took and surgeries I had had. It was quite a long process, very detailed. She entered all my answers in a computer system and left after the interrogation, leaving me alone in the room.

After some minutes, a tall man entered the room and introduced himself. "Hi, my name is Dr. Willy. I believe you are Fernando? How can I help you?"

"Hi, Dr. Willy, nice to meet you. Yes, my name is Fernando," I said. "I am a transgender woman and my preferred name is Manuela, although I am wearing men's clothes today. I could not come presenting as a girl because of businesspeople that are here visiting me."

"That is perfectly all right Manuela, we shall call you this from now on, I will make sure that your preferred name is registered. We get that all the time."

"I have here a letter from Dr. Carol Clark. I need to see an endocrinologist to start hormone replacement therapy, and I heard that this care center has experience in the field and can help me," I said.

"Okay, I understand. Well, I am a internist, but I have been doing this type of therapy for a while now. This clinic is very well known for this treatment, and we have quite a lot of experience here," Dr. Willy said as I handed him the letter. He read it and said, "Okay, we have to start by giving you a blood test and examining you. Make an appointment for the blood test on the way out and another appointment in two weeks to see me and discuss the results. You will see in a couple of months that you will be another person."

"I cannot wait until I start my new life. I am very excited," I said. "Thank you, Dr. Willy. I will see you soon."

I made my appointment for the blood test for the following morning and went to meet my colleagues at the mall.

The next morning, a very nice nurse took my blood, and then I left for a day of sightseeing with my business associates.

This was the beginning of a very large transition for me, with all its emotions and incredible changes. In the past I had lived all the time as Fernando, playing a big game, a game that had absorbed my entire life so that I didn't know where I was anymore. I always sought comfort by wearing women's clothes—but when I was alone, hiding from other people. Now that I had started to admit to myself who I was, there was an immediate sense of relief because there would be no more lies, no more hiding—well, at least not from myself. There was another world to conquer, the world around me, so it was truly the beginning of a big change.

Two weeks later, I came back to see Dr. Willy; I remember that it was July 30. This time I came in as Manuela, fully dressed as a girl. There was the same interrogation as before, getting weighed, answering questions about my moral fiber, sexual orientation, and of course sexually transmitted infections or the possibility of catching them. My sexual activity could be described as nonexistent, so it was not a difficult thing to answer.

When I came to the care center, my heart was pounding very strongly. I was showing myself to Dr. Willy as a girl for the first time.

Ten minutes after I arrived, the nurse called in a loud voice, "Fernando."

There were a lot of people in the waiting room, some apparently women, some men, but I appeared to be the only transgender woman, and was not very passable at the time. I felt a great deal of negative emotion as I was called Fernando in front of everybody. I almost expected the other patients to laugh in my face; I felt an incredible amount of shame. All the same, I followed the nurse back to the examination room.

After several minutes Dr. Willy came into the room and said, "Oh, you look very pretty." He was trying to be nice, I suppose. "Soon all the guys will be after you."

I grinned and said, "Hi, Dr. Willy. Well, let's see what happens."

"First of all, what is your preferred name?"

"My female name is Manuela."

"Okay, I will put this name in our system in brackets so that everybody knows what to call you in the future."

"Really? That is so nice." This news made me feel quite astonished and happy.

"So that is taken care of. We like to respect our patients," he said. "Let's see the results of the blood tests. Hmm, your cholesterol is high, we have to do something about it, and your testosterone is extremely high. No worries, though; we will get that under control."

"Okay, please explain what do I have to do," I said.

"I don't think you need any cholesterol medicine. It could be that it will go down by itself; you should try to lose some weight."

"I am losing weight. I already almost lost twenty pounds. I am going to a weight loss center and have a very strict diet, about eight hundred calories per day right now."

"Okay, that is good. Let's see how it goes. For your HRT I am going to give you two medicines. One is a testosterone blocker; this will reduce quite significantly the testosterone levels in your body, meaning you will have almost no male sex hormones anymore. The second medicine is an estrogen called estradiol; this will increase your estrogen, the female sex hormone. We will start in a small doses, and in three months we will test your blood to see what the changes are."

"Wow, I feel very excited! Finally some progress."

"Yes, but be careful. The effect of these hormones is quite significant. You will be quite emotional; sometimes you will probably lose control of your emotions—that is, until you are used to them. You will go through a second puberty, but this time as a woman. The estrogen will give you smoother skin, your body hair will not grow so fast, and you will start to develop a female figure with breasts and curves," said Dr. Willy.

"I cannot wait. I have been waiting for this all my life," I said.

"I can imagine. I have other patients that have gone through major changes, you will see. Just be very careful. Later you will do some plastic surgery, and some of these surgeries are irreversible. Always consult with your healthcare team before you make those decisions."

"I will certainly do so. I understand that major changes are coming," I said.

"For the first year or so we will take a blood test every three months to see how your hormone levels are reacting, then we will make it every six months. So the testosterone blocker is called 'spiro,' and the estrogen is called estradiol. You will take them both orally, but please take them two times a day, one in the morning and one in the evening." Dr. Willy typed out the prescription on the computer. "When you leave, the nurse will give you the prescription."

"Okay, wow, finally," I said.

"Yes. So, your pharmacy will have your prescription for six months," said Dr. Willy. "Another question: how is your sex life? Are you active?"

"Well, not really. I am married, but it has not worked for some time. It is very hard to have an erection," I said.

"It looks like you have erectile dysfunction, which is quite common at your age. I can give you some samples of a medicine called Cialis, see if it works."

"Okay, that sounds great." I stood up and shook hands with Dr. Willy.

"Okay, sexy lady. I will see you in three months, please make an appointment."

I walked out of the doctor's office in extasy and went through the corridor to customer service, where I picked up my prescription and made an appointment for the blood test and my next visit to Dr. Willy.

Wow, finally starting HRT! The creation of a new person, of Manuela, was starting there and then. I drove directly to my pharmacy, where I was supposed to pick up the prescription.

For a transgender person the starting date of HRT is like a second birthday, a day to remember, the day where many dreams come true and finally the change into your real self starts. For me, it feels like the way to Nirvana.

I was so excited on the drive to the pharmacy that I even forgot that I was wearing women's clothes until I parked. As I entered the pharmacy, not many people were looking at me, but I had this feeling that everybody was looking, like there were alarms going off, but that was only my feeling of guilt.

She approached the prescription counter and waited a couple of minutes for a pharmacy technician to come over.

"Do you have a prescription?" the pharmacy tech asked and looked at me in a very peculiar way.

"Yes," I said and handed her the prescription.

"Okay, Mr. Marques, do you have health insurance?" said the girl in a kind of mocking way.

"Sure, just a second," I said as I opened my purse, looked for my health insurance card, and gave it to her.

The girl went to the computer, entered all the information, and came back to the counter. "We do have the medicine here, but either you will have to come later or you can wait twenty minutes while we prepare it for you. When do you want to pick it up?"

"I will wait, no issue," I said and started to wander around the store and see the different products they had to offer while I waited.

I was really excited; I had waited all my life for this moment. About thirty years before, I had seen on a crossdressing website some formulas for so-called 'natural hormones,' medicines that were sold over the counter in the US like black cohosh, wild yam, and others. At that time I couldn't find them where I lived in Switzerland, so as soon as I had the opportunity to go to the US, I bought as much as I could and started experimenting. The results were slow, but they were there. Later I had heard about an artificial product that was given to transgender women in the nineties called Diane. It was a baby pill with some testosterone blockers, and one needed a prescription for it. I managed at the time to get one month's dose, but that was it, no more, so I went back to over-the-counter products. In the meantime, I was living in France and found a reliable source in her local pharmacy. But this time, on July 30, was the real thing, with an actual doctor's prescription and regular testing.

Time went by, and there was a voice calling, "Fernando, please come to pharmacy."

I was very embarrassed, but I went to the pharmacy counter. "Hi, my name is Fernando," I said to the girl, fully aware of my female clothes. "I am picking up my prescription."

"Yes, it is finished, but first some security questions. What is your birthdate?"

"August thirteen," I said.

"Okay, here you have your medicine, Fernando," said the technician. "You have to take two spironolactone tablets a day and four estradiol tablets a day. It is recommended that you take one half in the morning and the other half in the afternoon."

As I listened to her drone on, I was thinking, 'I cannot believe it! I did it, girl. I officially started HRT. This is just the start of my new life. I now have a new birthday.'

In the first days after I started taking my prescriptions there was no big change; it came about slowly but surely. I believe the first effect was my mood and the feelings, and then the desired effects took place, meaning my nipples got even more sensitive, my breasts started to grow, my skin started got softer, my body hair grew less coarse, and the weight distribution in my body changed. These physical effects took some weeks to come about, but they were there and there was progress. The effects of hormones are amazing. It is a slow but steady progression that is very personal depending on a person's age and weight and many other factors. Psychological changes due to the hormones are another astonishing thing. All of a sudden, I was experiencing moods that I hadn't known existed. I got very talkative and more aware of what was going around me.

I was going regularly to support groups to listen and talk with my transgender colleagues and friends. One of those Fridays it was my time to introduce myself, and I said, "Hi, I have had my first month on HRT."

All the group clapped their hands in approval.

"And how do you feel, Manuela?" asked one person.

"Well, I am starting to feel more at home. First I have no aggression. I feel very calm and relaxed, just sometimes I am very emotional. The other day I was watching a movie, and I could not stop crying. It was beautiful, all those emotions coming out. I was always a bit emotional, but never like that. The only thing is that I sometimes have quite a lot of pain in my breasts."

"That is normal," Ellen, one of the more advanced girls in the group. "It is because your breasts are growing; you will see quite soon. Welcome to your second puberty, just this time it will be quite different from the first one. Put your seatbelt on and enjoy the ride."

"I will," I said.

"Just be careful. This ride is very personal and can be difficult," Ellen carried on. "Transgender people are persecuted; they are victims of violence. It is not an easy thing to do. Some of us are more lucky then others; some are passable and they mix well, though this is not always the case. Getting your identification papers right is quite an experience as well; you will see if you get there. The way we present and act is very important; people will judge you on that and it is a big giveaway if you do not present correctly. And the other thing is the money you spend changing—new clothes, the health aspects, then you have hair removal and the surgeries. All are big costs and sometimes very painful. As we say, it is easier to be born a woman than to become one. Believe me, you have to be motivated to do it all."

"Yes, I understand. I am already in the process of losing weight and trying to get a suitable wardrobe to be passable. At the moment I am not living as a woman yet, but I am slowly getting there," I said.

"But Ellen is right. It is not an easy process, and the support from family and friends is so important," said another girl, Britney. She was in her late forties, quite passable, with the beautiful look of a mature woman. "I transitioned twenty years ago, had my gender reassignment surgery eighteen years ago, and lived for six years as a woman. Then my family made a lot of pressure for me to take over the business, so I had to go back to life as a man. I married a woman, though we never consummated the marriage—I do not have the parts—but we are still married, with many problems. But that is what my family wanted me to do. They could not admit that I was a woman; they made me as a boy, and they wanted me to always be one. Now I am at the point that I cannot live as a man anymore; the pain of the binders to hide my breasts and the mental pain of having to play this drama is unbearable. I cannot take it anymore. I decided to leave my family, start my new life, and go far away from them because they do not accept me. I don't know where I am going to sleep tonight, but I just want to be myself, start my real life, restart hormones, and stop my depression." She carried on. "When I stopped estrogen, and since my body does not produce testosterone anymore, I had terrible mood swings and of course hot flashes. All these years without hormones were very difficult; I had many periods of depression and headaches. I want to make a stop to it, and that is now."

It was always interesting to hear the stories of other transgender people, both trans men and trans women. Those stories are so varied, but most of them have not been so fortunate. Hardship and homelessness are a difficult but all-too-common phase.

"It is very interesting that many people see transgender people as making a choice about their gender. What I mean is that I get the comment that I chose to be a girl," said Ellen. "Well, this is not true. I did not have the choice to become a woman; the people that raised me failed to accept me as a woman and forced me to grow as a man because my genitals were male genitals but my brain and my feelings were always those of a woman. The only choice we have is to be happy and admit to ourselves who we really are. I think this is the reason why we feel so much better when the hormones in our bodies correspond to our true gender identity. You feel good and at home. And that is the same for transgender women and transgender men, the same."

"You are so right, Ellen," said Patrick, a very good-looking African American transgender man. "There was no choice for me but to become the man I am today. I was always like this, just my family refused to admit that I was not the girl they wanted me to be. I was going through lots of depression; I tried to commit suicide many times. Once I decided not to get out of bed for two weeks; it was total depression. Since I have had my T, my testosterone treatment, I feel so much better. I want to live, I want to fight to be myself, I am alive. Now I go regularly to the gym, I got myself a very manly body, had top surgery to remove my breasts, and now I am thinking of getting bottom surgery, but it is very expensive. I transitioned five years ago, and there is no going back for me, that is for sure. I am married to a cis woman; we are thinking now of adopting a child, we want a child. Testosterone brings many changes. Our voices go deeper, we start to have hair on our bodies and faces. The mental changes are quite extreme as well but in the opposite direction of a trans woman. For health reasons and to reduce the amount of medicines we take, you should really remove the ovaries, meaning to getting a hysterectomy."

"Well trans women have to get an orchidectomy to remove the testicles and stop testosterone production. That is the equivalent of that surgery," added Ellen.

"This is a very interesting theme," Dr. Clark chimed in. "HRT in both cases from male to female or female to male is a big challenge, and unfortunately still not a science. There is a lot of trial and error, and I recommend starting slowly, since the good doctors don't have all the answers. And mostly a regular blood sample is needed to see if all is going in the right direction. Mostly try to have a doctor that has experience with transgender people; it is still very rare to find one."

"Yes, is there anyone you recommend?" said another girl, June. "I was going to a gynecologist in Deerfield Beach, but I don't want to go there anymore. They are mistreating me because I am a transgender person, and I do not feel at ease anymore. I started hormones two month ago; she gave me a progesterone cream that I use on my skin, but I don't see much change and I have to say I don't trust too much what she is doing to me. I believe that she is using something that cis women use in menopause, but it's not for transgender women. And since I started this treatment I feel that I am putting weight."

"There is a clinic in Fort Lauderdale—Care Center I believe it is called. They have a good reputation for treating transgender people. I believe that some of you go there," said Dr. Clark.

"Yes, I go there," I chimed in, "and I seem to get good treatment. I have some oral medicine, spiro and estradiol, but if I understand this is quite standard in our community."

"Well, there are alternatives," said Ellen. "There are patches of estradiol and even shots. Many girls have the shots. The patches seem to be expensive, and you know not everybody has health insurance. I believe the cheapest is the oral pills, but it has its drawback to the stomach, because you are taking this on a long-term basis, literally all your life. But different doctors have different views. I have seen some people taking progesterone, but not many, and they all complain about weight gain, but it is very good for breast growth, and I believe for the hips as well. I have a weekly injection; it suits me very well. I had an orchy, so don't need spiro anymore."

"Ellen, where do you go for your medicine?" asked another younger girl.

"Well, girl, you know I am a veteran, as a matter of fact a Vietnam veteran, so I go to the VA in Miami. They have quite a lot of transgender people, and they know what they are doing," said Ellen.

"Wow," said the younger girl. "Veteran and transgender? That is incredible."

"Well," answered Ellen, "the military is a very big attraction for transgender people, both trans men and trans women. Transgender men go there as butch girls because they want to prove that they are tough guys, and many come out as guys. The trans women go to the army to prove to the world that they are men and not women; many of them fall into depression and learn their true identity. The same for gay men in the army; many movements have been started there. A very famous one was the Don't Ask, Don't Tell movement. How many guys went into the army to prove to themselves that they were straight men and came out as gay or transgender? A lot. In the army it has become a real culture. So don't be shocked about the amount of transgender women that are veterans. I believe the biggest institution for gay people in the US is the army."

"Yes," said another girl named Palmella. She was a veteran and had spent all of her life in the army. "The Don't Ask Don't Tell movement in the army started because there were questions about gender identity and sexual orientation. People were answering what they thought was right and not necessarily what they felt. Some people were murdered as homosexual and called 'fags,' and many were in the army. This movement was present for almost two decades, until homosexual people were accepted in the military, and that was quite a surprise."

"Hi, girls and boys, our time is over, and we have to stop the group. If you want get together for dinner, there are some diners we usually go to," said Dr.

Clark. "Please help me to put the chairs together and give some money to the center. They are supporting us with the room, and it is a charitable institution."

With those words, the support group ended. Everybody stood up, helped put the chairs in the right place, and all the individual conversations started. A group of people decided to go to a local diner, and I decided to go with them as usual.

Going to a restaurant when you have just started to transition is an issue. Manny issues are at stake here; on the one hand you are probably not very passable, making a target for other people, and comments and funny looks from others is not exactly what you want. On the other hand, your self-confidence and esteem are low, so by definition you think that everyone is looking and pointing at you. So, after these support group meetings, we would always go to LGBTQ-friendly places, and since we were in South Florida, Wilton Manors is the preferred place to be.

Coming Home to Venus

Becoming My Real Self

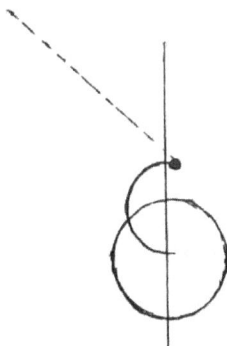

"Your real self - the 'I am I' - is master of this land, the ruler of this empire. You rightfully have power and dominion over it, all its inhabitants, and all contained in its realm."

Robert Collier

I felt just like all the other transgender girls and guys who had come before me, and I always said, "It is easier to be born a girl than to become one; obviously it's similar for transgender guys."

I sometimes thought I had to be completely nuts to go through this transition. I don't really think that people realize all the pain, trouble, danger, risk, and sometimes losses you go through to achieve it. Some face more than others, but for all of us it is a tremendously big change, and why do we do this? The answer is very simple: just to feel right; to look in the mirror and see myself and not some kind of weird person. Not to feel depressed and sad like I did for most of my life, but instead to think progressively and positively. And we go through all of this despite the risk of losing everything, the risk of discrimination, the risk of being turned out, and even being brutally treated. Yes, despite all this, if you are a real transgender person, transition is the only alternative; it is the only way to go, to be at truth with oneself, to stop your internal battle of hating yourself, and to evolve to the next step. Society does not always understand, although it is much better now. When I see statements like, "It was his choice to become a woman," I just feel sadness for the poor, ignorant person that said it.

In the beginning of my transition, when I was not really out of the closet, I developed a kind of ritual to go out as a woman. I would leave the house in my usual male clothes and female underwear, and would change in the car. Initially I would do this only to go to support groups, to see my therapist, and to go to the doctor. When my daughter, Victoria, left for college, I started to live as a woman at home, but I would get dressed as a man to go out, even shopping. Changing from one gender to the other and back again was proving to be a difficult emotional matter, for me and for the people around me, so I decided to present myself full time as a girl, meaning going shopping, to the supermarket, to see friends and family as my real self. In other words, I came out of the transgender closet.

I had an eight-step plan to follow. First, I would ensure that I was passable; second, I would work on self-confidence; third, I'd make sure my personal documentation corresponded to my image; fourth, come out as a woman with my friends and family; fifth, come out to my business colleagues and network; sixth, increase my degree of confidence; seventh, organize my new life financially and emotionally; and the last step was the complete affirmation into womanhood, the final surgery. That was always the goal, to be a complete woman, and to have the final touch of surgery that makes that possible. For a long time my mind was set on a compromise, though, as I had a cis-gender heterosexual partner and she had her needs. As a matter of fact, this is a very personal issue, and many transgender people have to make different perceptions and decisions about their romantic life as they transition.

Becoming passable is an important goal for every transgender person, both male-to-female and female-to-male.

"What is your definition of passable for a transgender person?" asked the therapist in the transgender support group.

After a short pause a woman named Heather said, "For me it means that you can go out as your real self without raising unwanted attention. Meaning I am a transgender woman and when I go out people recognize me as a woman, they talk to me as a woman and don't misgender me. In the transgender community we call it 'to be clocked' when someone looks at you and recognizes you are transgender."

"I agree with you," said Jess, "but I want to be sexy as a woman. I want men to want me and feel that they are attracted to me. I like to flirt with them and be desired."

"Oh my, you live dangerously," said Heather. "Well we are all different, I suppose. For me just to be respected as a woman is enough; being possessed is not my thing."

"I suppose we are all different as far as sexual expectations are concerned, but that is a sex issue, not a gender issue," said Tom, a transgender man. "I agree with Heather, to go shopping, to a restaurant, at work, and to be respected as my true self is my goal. I want to feel safe and not be misgendered."

"I agree with Heather and Tom, too," I said, "but there are so many things to be done before you achieve the passable stage. It also depends on your age and the level of hormones you take or have taken. Younger girls usually get passable more quickly; if they start before puberty they look really great very quick because their testosterone has not really taken effect."

"I believe that there are many factors in how much you are passable," said Heather. "Age is certainly a factor, how long you have been on hormones is another, then how many surgeries you have done, but this is only the physical aspect of your looks. Another thing that has to be taken into consideration is your behavior, the way you present yourself, and your voice. For the people that transition later in life they have to catch up with the lifetime of learning that cis people go through."

"Yes, I have seen many crossdressers that look quite good but behave like men; even if they sound very convincing, they are still not passable," I said. "On the other hand, older girls that don't look like Miss World but behave and very often sound very feminine are certainly passable. After all, many cis women are not incredibly beautiful; some don't take much care of themselves either. For trans men, I believe the effect of hormones is more important to be passable because of hair growth, and to a certain point the voice change."

"Don't forget that many of us started as crossdressers or drag queens," said Jess. "But I agree that we are very different from them. As I see it, crossdressers are men wearing women's clothes. They feel like men and behave like men; most are attracted to women, and many get sexually aroused when they wear female clothes. Drag queens are similar, but they are mostly gay and do it to earn money and get laid."

"I agree with you, and by the way, did you see how some drag queens hate transgender women. Some drag queen shows don't even accept transgender people, or treat them like shit," I said. "As a woman, I must say I sometimes feel offended by very exaggerated drag queens. Their looks are too hectic, very artificial. Sometimes it not far from a mockery to women."

"When we talk about passable, we should also take into consideration non-gender-conforming people and nonbinary people that identify with both traditional genders. Mostly they are not passable in both genders at the same time, and it is really difficult to integrate them," said Tom. "But they deserve our love and respect, and at least I respect them."

"I believe that for many of us the goal is not only to be passable, but to go one step further and integrate completely into the gender that we are supposed to be," I said, "meaning the gender that God gave us mentally, so you correct the body to achieve your true self. I believe that this is the way I want to go."

Losing weight and HRT were early parts of my transformation process. HRT made slow but steady and important changes in my mind and body. The rest was all about learning how to dress, to put on makeup, and to evoke ladylike manners.

It was time now for me to start living my truth on a daily basis, meaning presenting and doing all things as a woman. Slowly but surely, I started going out as a girl to restaurants, supermarket, bars, shopping, and of course to regular transgender support group meetings. Three months after I started hormones, there was an important meeting for the transgender community. It was the first time that I was going fully out and the beginning of me living almost 100 percent as a woman.

One day as I was transitioning, I got up early, put on a beautiful, two-piece, red dress, did my makeup, put on a terrible, white wig and some high heels and left the house to go down the street to the weight-loss center. It was the first time that I was going there dressed as a girl. I got out of the car and walked directly through the door.

"Good morning, how can I help you?" asked Monika, the receptionist on the other side of the counter.

"Hi, Monika, I am coming in for my shot," I said.

"Okay, what is the name?" said Monika.

"Oh, you mean you do not recognize me? It's Manuela Marques," I said.

"Oh my God! I see, I had never seen you as a woman, and now I recognize you because of your voice. You look amazing, Manuela. Let me get your file and let's have your shot," said Monika.

"Yes, I am going to a meeting in Fort Lauderdale, and anyway it was high time that I start to come here as my real self. So you are the first person in the weight-loss center to see me as I really am," I said.

I followed Monika into the exam room, where I was given my typical weight-loss injection.

"How is everything going? I see you are not traveling at the moment," Monika said.

"Yes, only for a couple of weeks, then I have to go to California for some interesting projects. Business is very slow at the moment, but there are some projects for Tesla that we are pursuing. We will see how that turns out," I said.

After the shot, I drove to Weston, Florida, where I took part in a Conference. I registered as Ella, and I spent the day listening to different speeches on topics such as how to look more feminine, makeup, security as a transgender person, being transgender in the workplace, and most important for me, facial feminization surgery and sex reassignment surgery. It showed me that this world was getting organized but still had a lot of issues. At that time there was an area for exhibitors at the conference, and I found a wonderful older lady selling wigs.

"Hi, I am looking for a nice wig. Do you have anything for me? Something in a whitish color," I said.

"Sit down here, gorgeous, and let me see what I can find for you." She went to the back of her booth and came back a few minutes later with three pieces, all whitish in color. "Okay, I have three units for you to try. The first one is actually not really white; it's a mixture of blonde and white and is straight hair down to the shoulders. It is a synthetic fabric from a quality producer. Let's try it." She took off the wig I was wearing and put this one on my head.

Coming Home to Venus

This wig was like putting a plastic bag on my head. It was very hot, not something to wear the whole day. "I am not sure," I said. "It is very heavy, and it does not feel very good at all. I don't think that the blondish hair fits me either."

"Okay, let's try the next one. It is really white, as well synthetic. Anyway, all white wigs are synthetic because there is no real white hair on the market. Natural white hair is too thin and brittle, so either you have synthetic or a mix, but the natural hairs are from rhinoceroses," said the lady while taking away the blondish wig and putting the white wig on me.

"This looks like if I was an old lady, and it feels the same. It is very heavy and not really very comfortable."

"I have this one. It is more expensive. It's from Raquel Welch Wigs, and it is a very special synthetic. Let me know what do you think."

The wig was white in a lengthy page cut, with about thirty percent of dark brown hair mixed in.

"Wow, it is very comfortable, and my head feels quite good, like it can breathe. What is the price?" I asked.

"Well, for you, love, I can make it $650," said the lady.

"Do you mind if I show this piece to some friends before I decide? They are just down there."

"Sure, girl, take your time."

I walked over to Jamie, one of my therapists who was standing close by, and asked her, "Jamie, what do you think about my hairpiece?"

Jamie took a moment to study the wig and its effect on me "I think it fits you so well. The length and color really match you, although I would not go so white. A bit of color is good as well."

I asked two other friends, and they all seemed to like the way I looked. I went back to the lady and decided to purchase that piece. It was my favorite wig for a very long time.

Over the following days of the conference, I met with a lot of other transgender people and crossdressers and had a wonderful time. There was a book signing for *I Am Jazz* by Jazz Jennings; it was very interesting and I learned a lot about surgery, hormones, how to look better, and how to behave more like a woman. In the evening there was a big party, and I had some issues with some crossdressers that were clearly interested in having sex more than anything else. Well they tried to make some advances.

From those days on, there was no more wearing men's clothes unless I was going out for business and to visit clients. A few weeks after the conference, I went to Tampa with Jessica, the foster child that had been living in our house, to see Victoria, my daughter. During dinner Jessica went to the restroom, and I gathered my courage to come out to Victoria.

"I want to tell you something before you hear from someone else. I am transgender. I was born a boy, but I have a woman's mind and I am starting to live as a 100-percent woman," I said.

"What? I have heard about such people, but how do you know that you are a transgender?" asked Victoria.

"I was getting very depressed," I admitted, "and at the beginning of the year I decided to find an expert. Dr. Clark, my therapist, determined that I had gender dysphoria and I started in July 30 with hormone replacement therapy and have been living as a woman for some weeks now. I still present as a man for work, but that is it."

"Wow, I thought you were acting kind of weird, but I would never have expected it. Well, as long as you are happy," She said "But how long have you known this about yourself?"

"I have known about my feminine feelings since the age of five, and I have been hiding them ever since."

"That's a long time. Let's talk when we are alone, though. Jessica is coming back to the table," said Victoria.

Later Victoria and I had some very interesting talks about being and feeling. It created a strong bond between daughter and father—well, woman-father.

My next step was facial hair removal. After so many years with a beard, mustache, or some kind of facial hair, this was not an easy thing to do. On top of this, I only had white facial hair. Basically, there are only two ways to remove facial hair. One is by laser, where you attack the hair roots with a strong laser light. Unfortunately, this system only works with dark hair, not white hair. The only system that would work for me is called electrolysis,[v] which is the process of electrifying the individual roots of your facial hair with a special machine. I had seen some companies that did this. One in Texas offered a special service where two technicians take care of your face for many hours, but in one day you are done—that is, until some part of the hair comes back. It is a very painful procedure, though, and patients are put into anesthesia for the complete duration.

I decided to do this with a local person, so I started to look for one. Since electrolysis is a long-term process, prices are quite expensive, and most specialists give special discounts to transgender people.

Eventually I found a salon that offered electrolysis in West Boca. I went there and spoke with the gentleman at the desk.

"So, you are transgender. We have special rates for people like you, $80 per hour. Will that be okay?" asked the owner of the salon.

"Yes, that will be okay for me. But please tell me about the people that are doing this job and what systems you are using."

"We have very new machinery, and Maria, your electrologist, has been to a special school to learn how to do it very well. She is very fast and efficient; you will be very pleased," said the owner. "If you agree, let's go and see her. The first time you will pay individually; afterwards I ask you to pay by a package of ten."

"Okay, let's try this." I followed the man to the room where Maria was.

"Hi, Maria," said the owner as he opened the door. "You have a client for facial electrolysis; this is Manuela."

"Okay, let me see her face," said Maria with a very strong Eastern European accent. She turned on her very strong lights and held my face in her hands. "Let me see what you have around there. Okay, there is a lot of work to do. All your hair is white, and you have a lot of hair."

"Maria, can you make a session with Manuela now? Or do you have another customer?" asked the owner.

"Oh, I can do it now," said Maria. The owner left the room, and Maria told me where to lie down and get comfortable. "You are going to have a lot of pain," she warned me. "They just sent me to the training place for electrolysis, and I am starting to do it but I do not like this work. You need very good eyes, and this is not my strong point. And they want me to be very fast. They say that the amount of hairs removed per hour should be nine hundred, but this is so much. I cannot cope with it." Maria carried on complaining about everything, including her family, her boss—well, everything.

At the end of the session, I felt a lot of pain on my chin, where all the electrolysis had been done. I was not so happy with my experience, so as soon as I got home, I started looking for alternatives and came across another person called Lise-Anne

"Hi, my name is Ella. I am a transgender woman, and I am looking for electrolysis to finally get rid of my facial hair," I said as I entered Lise-Anne's office.

"Hi, Ella, nice to see you," said Lise-Anne. "You know about my rates, and since you will be coming regularly, I will give you a special discount." She guided me to a small room with a kind of a bed and a lot of special equipment. "Ella, lay down here and let me see your hairs."

I lay on that professional massage bed, and it was clear that my face had to go to the side where all the machines were.

"Let me look at you, girl," said Lise-Anne. She put on some very special magnifying glasses with a very intense diode light; it looked like a very sophisticated apparatus. Almost immediately she pulled back and clucked in her throat. "Who burned you? You have three burns on your chin. I promise you this will not happen with me. Sometimes these burns leave big holes that will not go away."

"Yes, I noticed them. It was from another person that was doing electrolysis on me. She really did not like what she did. That is why I am here."

"Okay, never forget: do not shave the area that you want to have electrolysis done on the day before you come here," she said. "Some of your hairs are quite easy to be taken out, so this is not an issue for today. You have a lot of hair, so I will try to work in different areas. I think you should come here once or twice a week, but it will take a while until all is clean."

"Okay, I understand," I said.

"Now let's see about getting the ideal strength for you. Please let me know if it is too painful." Lise-Ann put the needle inside my pores and sent an electric shock through them.

"I hardly noticed. You probably can go higher," I said.

"What about this level?" Slowly the ideal level of electricity was defined, and she started to clean all unwanted hairs, mostly white hairs, from my face.

I became very good friends with Lise-Anne and came to see her very regularly. It was not exactly a pleasure visit; it was always associated with pain. Sometimes she would put some numbing cream on my face because the areas she was treating were more sensitive than others. This mainly happened when there was some kind of nerve ending to get around.

Electrolysis is the only permanent hair removal, but sometimes you have to take out the hair multiple times for it to really disappear. Incredibly enough for me, sometimes some hairs that were white would come back black. I tried to remove those black hairs with a laser. It was okay, but after five or six weeks they would come back again.

Electrolysis on the face is painful but nothing compared to the pain when it is done between the legs, to be more specific in the perineal area. That has to be done before genital surgery. In this case it is only possible with a very strong local numbing cream.

Lise-Anne became my confidante and friend as well. We would have some evenings out together and share a lot about our lives.

The remaining hair removal I did in a very classical way, by shaving. Unlike facial hair, body hair reacts very well to hormones, meaning that as testosterone was not present in my body anymore, my body hair disappeared as well, becoming thinner and thinner over time.

Living and presenting all the time as a woman, hygiene and presentation is so important, and it is not only in the facial and body hair, but the hair on top of your head that is extremely important. If you are a young transgender woman and therefore not so damaged by testosterone, then you will likely not have many issues. One just grows the hair, and with the hormonal change, things will get better very soon. If like me you wait sixty years to have your big change, things are very different. I had two main issues: my hairline had receded over the years, and I had a bald spot like a monk. On the back and the sides there was some hair that grew quite well with time but still was very thin.

Living with a wig is not very practical, so I started to look for alternatives. The first was to get a hair transplant, but this was quite expensive and took a while to grow. As I did my research, I found out that many older cis women have very thin hair and bald spots as well, so it is a general issue with age.

For a while I was using the beautiful white wig that I had bought at the conference, but then I decided to look a bit younger. I remembered that my mother had had beautiful, dark brown har, and my sister as well, so why shouldn't I do the same? I then found out about topper pieces, which are hair pieces you put in with special clips that stay put very well. They are natural hair, so they are neither hot nor uncomfortable. That was one of my biggest changes, going from white hair to dark brown with reddish undertones . It fit my look fantastically.

Later I started doing something even more incredible: I beaded the hair into position. This is incredible because it stays in place; you can sleep with it, go to the swimming pool, and live your complete, normal life with your topper piece in place. You have to tighten it up about once every four weeks. The issue is the cost and the fact that, with time, your own hair starts to thin at the place where you put the beads in so that the process becomes ineffective. I still use this system today, but sometimes I change to clips for a couple of months to let my hair grow.

Hair transplants are certainly encouraging. Living with a hairpiece is work and sometimes not ideal. There are many doctors for this type of procedure all over the world. In the US costs are high, but other countries such as Turkey have a very good reputation for quality surgery done at an affordable cost. This is something to study and look at the different possibilities.

The other concern when you are living life as a full-time woman is of course makeup and the way you present yourself.

Coming Home to Venus

"No person is your friend who demands your silence, or
denies your right to grow."
Alice Walker

I started to organize dinners for transgender people
and our friends. All these dinners were held in a
very nice restaurant called Rosie's in Wilton
Manors, the second-most LGBTQ-friendly town in
the US, so nobody really looked at us—that is,
unless someone ever deigned to go naked. This
town is regarded as a safe place and a place of
acceptance. So many people that would come out
for the first time as transgender would come to
those dinners.

One night there were about twenty transgender
people at the table, some very passable and some

barely recognizable as if they were in their preferred gender.

"I feel really bad. People keep misgendering me, all the time," a not so passable woman named Tina said to me.

"Oh, are you living full time as a girl?" I asked.

"Well, most of the time. You see, I have long hair, and I usually wear girlie shorts and shoes."

"Well, Tina, I don't want to be rude, but sometimes one has to do bigger effort to be more passable. There are many things one can do such as getting some advice from a specialist. I thought you were a genderfluid person myself, and being transgender is not something that is usually very easy for most people to understand," I said. "Don't forget, even cis women try to find out what their style is and make a lot of changes until they know how to present. Some are more feminine than others."

"Come on, Manuela, we are in Florida," said Rachel, another girl from the group. "Here everyone presents the way they want to present. There is total freedom."

"Yes, but you have to admit that in order to enhance your femininity and be more passable, you have to look at yourself and see what you want to emphasize in your body to be more feminine," I answered. "Everybody does that.

"And there are a lot of factors you have to take into consideration for the right presentation, for example, the right clothes, the right manners, perfume or scent, and others. For example, I cannot stand a transgender girl who does not position her legs correctly, meaning that she always has her legs wide open, mainly with a skirt, showing her undies. Worst is when she crosses her legs like a guy and you can see that there is a large package between her legs. That is not very feminine at all."

"You are probably right, Manuela, but the important thing is that she feels good," said Rachel.

"Yes, but then don't complain about being misgendered," I said. "Right?"

Acceptance is such an important thing for any transgender person. Some people think that transgender people occupy the lowest position on the food chain, so they can be abused and taken advantage of. In some states in the US, transgender people cannot go to the bathroom of their chosen gender even if they are very passable. The risk is being put in prison, having to paying money to get out, and going to the risk of being abused or even raped. A trans woman, even if she looks very beautiful, would have to go to a male prison or be in a solo confinement, if it's available.

But what does it take to achieve acceptance? Well, we should not only look at transgender people but also try to learn from cis people. Many of them have the same issues of fears and acceptance, transgender people tend to highly amplify then but acceptance issues and fears are feelings that everybody has.

At the beginning of my transition, I had a larger body with a big belly, which is not exactly feminine and attractive. Attractiveness is important for most transgender women. The first times that I dressed up as a woman, I did it in the car, without much space or light, and I was not very passable, a fact I was very much aware of. The clothes were not exactly nice and stylish, the makeup was horrible, and the rest, well, I had a lot of learning to do.

At that time, after the transgender meetings, we all used to go and have dinner at a restaurant in Wilton Manors that can be described as very tolerant. One of the first times in this place, there were about fourteen of us, mostly transgender, though some were therapists, and it was an occasion for them to be with transgender people and learn a bit about us.

Coming Home to Venus

"Wow, there are so many people here," I said to one of the other transgender girls. "I think the restaurant knows that many of us are transgender."

"Of course," answered one of the girls that seemed more passable. "We come here very regularly, and look at us. Some are quite passable, but for others it is not really the case. We look very mixed and different."

"Yes, I think you are right. I do not really feel like I am passable," I said.

"Don't worry, you will get there," said Ellen. "It is only a matter of time, hormones, and the will to get there. Some girls don't have as much will as others, but we are all different."

"Yes, I live as a man, come here to this meeting and stay for three days, but I don't want to stop my career," said Felicia. "I usually bring a friend who does my makeup and like this I experience my femininity, but I am too scared to become full time. I have my job. I don't want to lose it, and I have a nice life that I want to preserve and enjoy."

"I can understand that. I am not sure what I want to do, but I want to find out about myself and see where it goes," I said. "I am in the beginning of my therapy. I have to understand myself, but somehow I want to look better as a girl."

Coming Home to Venus

Probably one of the major changes that allowed me to come into my own as a girl was at the Southern Comfort Conference. It was a big opportunity for many things, first to be there in my female clothes, in an environment that was acceptable and friendly; second to meet a lot of people like myself. It was also an opportunity to try different things, like makeup tutorials and to hear what doctors were proposing to transgender people.

The Southern Comfort Conference is quite the event for the international transgender and crossdressing communities. This event started many years ago in Atlanta, Georgia; it was a great success, with hundreds of people in attendance. It was the opportunity for crossdressers to dress up for several days in a row, to be together, talk to each other, and to go out to evening events. For transgender people it was the opportunity to attend different lectures with themes ranging from medical, to work-related, legal advice, vocal training, and many things that we were interested to hear. There were quite a lot of events as well with prominent people, good food, and nice speeches.

This conference moved to Fort Lauderdale by the time I went there. At that time I already had spent some months on HRT and I had lost a lot of weight. I started to look more passable, and I had bought some nice dresses online. The first event I went to was a makeup tutorial. It was quite an event. All of us went to Sephora, where the salesgirls showed us how to use foundation, eye makeup, lip gloss, and gave us other makeup tips. It was a nice opportunity to have some good advice from makeup experts and to buy some products based on this advice.

The remaining lectures were also very interesting: facial feminization from a famous plastic surgeon in Florida, showing the differences between male and female faces, and what type of interventions can be done; gender reassignment surgery, for both trans men and trans women, what had to be done to get your genitals to correspond to yourself. There were some photos that were quite shocking of the before, during, and after of surgical interventions.

Vocal training was another theme, how to position your voice to have the right pitch, how the vocabulary of men and women differs, as well as everything to present your body in the way that you want it to function. Other presentations were more about the person, workplace acceptance, and safety.

There are many conferences and support groups that can help transgender people with advice during their transition. Some advice is about appearance, some is about surgeries, and some is about social issues including transitioning at work.

Some very interesting speakers have made amazing presentations about transitioning on the job.

"Appearance is a very important part of life when you are working, and that is for anybody. It does not matter if you are a cis woman, a transgender woman, a cis man, or a transgender man. Yes, it depends on the type of job that you have and if you have direct contact with customers or not. When we talk about appearance, we mean the way we dress and the way we present ourselves. Being transgender, it is a bit more complicated than with cis women; one thing is the acceptable dress code for the job, the other is how you appear as a person," said Ashley, a transgender activist and wonderful motivational speaker at the conference. "Transitioning on the job is a process that takes some time, and we should not skip steps to arrive at a good result. One of the most important steps is acceptance, so what does this mean? There are two types of acceptance that are so important. One is self-acceptance, meaning accepting yourself, and the other is acceptance by others. Self-acceptance is sometimes very difficult for transgender people. Think of all the times you've asked yourself, 'Am I passable?'"

This resonated with me very strongly when I heard it. One of the first times I went out to a restaurant as a woman was with a very good friend of that came to Florida from Switzerland for a visit. We went to a very well-known American restaurant chain. I was wearing a jeans skirt, a red top with a golden zipper, some medium-size heels, golden jewelry, and carrying a black bag. My makeup was not extreme, but correct and feminine. I had on my short, white page wig, and I actually looked very passable and feminine.

I parked the car, and both Margarida and I stepped out.

"How do I look?" I asked her.

"Don't be nervous, girl, you look great. Just relax and enjoy," she said.

Both slowly walked into the restaurant.

"Oh my God, it's full of people," I said. "We should go somewhere else."

Margarida laughed. "Don't be afraid. You will survive it and laugh about it later."

My heart was beating very fast, and I was in such a degree of stress that I started to sweat.

"How many are you?" said the hostess at the entry of the restaurant.

"We are two people," I said with a somewhat masculine voice.

"Okay, under what name?" said the hostess as she looked more intensely at me.

"Manuela," I said. This time I tried to pitch my voice higher, only succeeding in going into a forced level that was not really very feminine either.

"It's a thirty-minute wait," said the hostess and gave me a black calling machine.

"Thank you," I said as I headed outside with Margarida. "These waiting times are usually shorter than they say."

As we stood outside, we started to talk about friends, my transition, and a thousand and one things. I was so nervous, though, that I was not really concentrated on our conversation. 'Oh my God,' I remember thinking. 'That girl is looking at me. She is very nice, but I am sure that she already understood that I am trans. What shall I do?'

Well, the very nice-looking girl was in her early thirties, and she just happened to literally scan everybody that was waiting at the front door of the restaurant.

'Look at those two young boys. They are laughing, I am sure it is about me,' came my next thought, even though it was clear they were laughing at their lives and their friends, nothing to do with me. Most people waiting outside were thinking and talking with their friends and acquaintances, worrying about their own lives and not paying attention to me.

Finally, the black alarm vibrated and our table was ready. We followed the hostess to our table, where I carried on with my suspicious thoughts. 'I hope I am safe with the people next to my table. Oh my God, it is like being a model in a fashion show—everyone is watching me. No, Manuela, get a hold of yourself. It's probably me being paranoid.'

We were already eating when all of a sudden some people came to the table next to ours. I recognized them immediately as the parents of a friend of Victoria, my daughter.

'Oh no,' I inwardly groaned. 'It's Antonia and her husband. I hope they will not see me, how embarrassing.'

I must have made a very scared face as I had those thoughts. Margarida immediately noticed and asked, "What is going on? Is something wrong?"

"Well, you see the couple at the table next to ours?" I whispered. "They are the parents of a very good friend of Victoria. I know them very well, and I hope they don't see me."

Margarida was laughing. "Do you really think that these people will recognize you with your makeup, wig, and feminine clothes? Come on, give yourself a break. If they do, what do you have to lose? You are coming out, right? They are not going to kill you, you know! I know you have been on the edge the whole night, but you do not need to be so nervous."

Margarida was so right, and so was Ashley: self-acceptance is really the most difficult of all. The way you think you present is not the only issue concerning self-acceptance for a transgender person. Many years of guilt are not exactly something you can overcome in one minute; it takes time and a lot of courage. Your inner demons must leave you, so there is some intense work to do. It's worth it, though. You need that self-acceptance because it's the basis for self-confidence and success.

Acceptance from others is something else, a very vast subject that is not only a transgender issue. Cis people have acceptance issues as well.

"Acceptance from others," said Ashley in her presentation, "is driven by how people perceive you, and for trans or cis people, it is the same thing. Just it is more difficult to arrive at a suitable status if you are transgender. Acceptance does not mean that you have to be perfect; it means that you have to be suitable for what you are doing, and that people take you at your true value. You don't have to present in the same way if you are a salesperson of luxury goods that you would if you worked as an assistant in a factory. For a transgender person, passable means that you look like and are at ease with the gender you identify with.

Voice is another important giveaway for any transgender person. Many do not want to change their voice, and we should respect that, but some find it very unattractive if you look like a fantastic female model and sound like a redneck man. There are many factors to be taken in a vocal feminization.[vi] One is the pitch. Some people can change that through surgery, though it is not an easy thing to do; others change their pitch by training with voice therapists. But one must remember that a feminine voice is not only about pitch but also about the way you talk, the articulation, timber, and the words you choose are all possible issues. As usual, perfection is not always asked for; many cis woman have low voices as well, so just remember, that the number of imperfections is a strong giveaway. In the US and in many countries, there is a large amount of specialists on vocal feminization; one very famous one in the US is Kate Perez.[vii] She really works wonders with her students. I followed Kate on the internet and had some training from a local therapist to work on my voice.

HRT already starts many of these changes for most people, but special surgeries such as facial feminization surgery (FFS), breast augmentation, tummy tuck, or breast removal for the guys are options to be taken in consideration, according to how much can you pay.

Procedures

"But you can only lie about who you are for so long without going crazy."
Ellen Wittlinger

In fact, I was contemplating some surgeries. Soon after I started transitioning, I began investigating my options. The first surgery I was looking for was facial feminization surgery (FFS).[viii]

One morning I drove to an FFS specialist in South Florida.

In the waiting room, a nurse handed me two binders full of pictures and said, "Here, please look at some of the work Dr. Gen has done. These are before-and-after pictures."

One binder was dedicated to cis women's before-and-after pictures; the other was full of transgender women. I started to look at the photos in detail, and it seemed that some women had quite amazing surgeries. As a result, they looked so young and beautiful but somehow lost their character. Meanwhile, others just had little changes done to their faces but remained themselves. I had already been living as a woman for one year, and sometimes I presented as a man, so a drastic change would not be acceptable. Looking at those pictures I regretted not having done this about thirty years before, so that I could present as a woman in my youth, as I was just starting out in the world of business.

"Hi, Manuela," said Dr. Gen as he opened the door to the waiting room. "Come with me. We are going to the examination room."

The examination room was a really white, clinical room, what you might expect from a first-class doctor.

"I saw the before-and-after pictures," I said as I followed him into it. "Some look really amazing, but I am not sure I want to go so extreme. I suppose I want to have something that is not too much."

"That should be no issue. We will start by taking some pictures of your face, I will make some recommendations, and then we can decide what to do," said the doctor.

One of his assistants entered the room with a large camera.

"Hi, Manuela," they said. "Please stand near the white wall. I want you to look at me straight on, at 90 degrees. Now move 45 degrees to your right." All told, she took five pictures of my face from practically every angle.

At the same time Dr. Gen was looking at me and making some notes. The assistant took the memory chip out of the camera and plugged it into a computer to show me all the pictures that she took of me.

"Okay," Dr. Gen said, "this is what I think you should do to your face. First I would do a forehead feminization, then do both your upper and lower eyelids. We could do your eyebrows as well, but we would have to remake your hairline. I would also suggest a rhinoplasty to make your nose smaller and more feminine. I would do something with the lips too. On the bottom part of the face you don't really need anything done."

"Wow, that sounds like a lot. Can you explain all the procedures that you are proposing? How do you do them?" I asked.

"Sure." Dr. Gen sat on a stool as he began explaining the procedures. "Let's start with the forehead feminization, or contouring. In men, the brow bone is slightly higher than for females, so we would shave this bone so that the face becomes more feminine. To get to the bone we make an opening at the back of the head so the scar will be underneath the hair, then bring the skin to the front to do the work. All of this is done with the patient fully anesthetized, and the pain goes away fast.

"You can do a brow lift as well. To do this, we would make an incision in the hairline to lift them. In your case, though, since your hairline doesn't have much hair, we would do a hair transplant to bring in more volume.

"You should also get eyelid surgery, or blepharoplasty. In your case it would help to open your eyes and make your eyes larger. I would do this surgery independently, whether you had facial feminization surgery or not. It is a simple surgery. There are the upper eyelids and the lower ones. On the top lids we make an insertion and remove the excess skin. In the lower lid we remove the fat. A rhinoplasty is to make your nose more feminine. In your case we would reduce the sides of your nose and retouch the bone, but not much."

"Yes, but Dr. Gen, doesn't it reduce someone's character if you change their nose?" I asked.

"Well, a bit certainly, but it's always a tradeoff. You can have beauty or retain your character, it's your choice. That applies to all the procedures."

"Yes, I suppose you're right. It applies to all people, transgender or cis, how they want to present themselves, how much can they afford, their pain tolerance... I suppose there are many things that have to be taken into consideration," I said. "I'll have to think about it."

I was unsure about how much surgery I wanted to do. Looking feminine was important to me, but there was no need to look twenty years old again. Otherwise it might look too fake.

I decided to see other doctors before deciding what to do in order to see what their propositions were. It was not so easy to find first -lass plastic surgeons that specialized in transgender people. I brought this question to my support group to see what others thought

"Finding the right doctor for the surgeries is not an easy task," said Ellen. "First you have to determine their general level of experience, then you have to find out if a surgeon specializes in a specific procedure before finding out how many transgender people they've treated. And then of course the regular question: Does health insurance cover this surgeon and procedure? This can be a big challenge for us, especially if you are under veteran's health insurance like I am."

"Yes, let's face it: for certain types of surgery, you can count on your hand the number of specialists available for specific transgender surgeries, but many claim that they can do something when in reality they cannot," answered Maribel.

"Oh yes, girls," I chimed in. "I can tell you a nice story about just how specialized they are. Some weeks ago I went to my regular doctor..."

And I told them the following story of a frustrating occurrence I'd had with healthcare.

"So Manuela," said Dr. Willy. "Your hormone levels seem to be quite good. How do you feel?"

"I am doing great, but sometimes I feel extremely tired and I see that my blood pressure is very low. What can I do?"

"That is most probably the effect of spiro. You could go around this if you had an orchiectomy done," he said. "This is the removal of the testicles. If you do this, you cannot produce testosterone anymore, so you will have the same testosterone level that a cis woman that gets from the thyroid."

"I have heard about this option many times, and I feel that it would be a great idea," I said. "They are always in the way and are a source of discomfort. Do you know who could do that procedure?"

"Most urologists can do it because they usually do so when men have cancer in the testicles," said Dr. Willy. "Go and see our recommended urologist and see what he says." And he gave me a referral to see a urologist.

The day came, and I went to the urologist. I arrived to a waiting room full of men. I was the only woman there, which made me feel very uneasy.

I was put in a small room where I waited for a while. After some minutes a middle-aged Indian woman arrived.

"Hi, I am Dr. Krishna," she said. "How can I help you?"

"Hi, Dr. Krishna, I was referred to you to have an orchiectomy," I said. Well, the answer came across like a big shock. The good doctor looked at me, waiting with a puzzled look on her face, so I carried on. "Yes, I am a transgender woman and I would like to have my testicles removed so that I do not produce testosterone anymore."

"Okay," she said. "I have removed some testicles, but mostly just for men with cancer. Just a second, I want to see something." And she left the room.

Half an hour passed with no signs of the good doctor. Then forty-five minutes and still nothing. I started to get impatient and tired of waiting. One hour of waiting and still nothing. I stood up, left the room to see the nurses, and said, "I am sorry, Dr. Krishna was going to come back and I am still waiting."

"Oh, I will see what it is!" said the nurse and went to an office with an open door. I could hear her say, "Dr. Krishna, your patient is asking for you."

"Oh, oh, oh!" The doctor got up and walked over to me. "Mrs. Marques, according to the World Professional Association for Transgender Health, you need one letter so that I can perform this operation. Do you have such a letter?"

"Yes, of course, but first one question: have you ever treated a transgender patient?"

"I will be honest with you: no. I had to phone a friend of mine that sent me to the WPATH website, and I took a long time trying to read it," she admitted. "It seems that there are a lot of things associated with treating a transgender patient."

"Okay, thank you for your honesty. Please give me some time to think of what to do next."

I left the building and went home, thinking, 'Do I really want to be Dr. Krishna's experiment? I somehow don't want to be cut by someone who is reading the instruction manual on the side.'

I looked into many other doctors until she found Dr. Green in Tampa, Florida, a plastic surgeon with experience with transgender patients. I made an appointment, and on the day I drove the four hours to Tampa and went out for lunch with Victoria.

"Papi, I want to come with you to see the doctor," my daughter said.

"Are you sure? It is probably going to be very detailed and not so nice," I warned her.

"Yes, but you are important to me and I would like to know what is going on."

"Okay, my love, you are always welcome."

We drove together to the surgeon's office.

When I handed the whole package of intake documents to the nurse, I said, "My daughter would like to be with me for the consultation. Is that possible?"

"Oh, that is so nice," she said with a smile, "a daughter that comes with her mother. I am sure it is possible. Just sit down, my colleague will be with you very soon."

Before long, we had been guided to a clean, white room by Dr. Green's head nurse.

"Please sit down," she said. "Dr. Green is coming very soon."

She left the room, and within one or two minutes she returned with Dr. Green, a very handsome man.

"So what brings you here?" said Dr. Green as we all sat down.

I introduced myself and my daughter, and Dr. Green asked about my transition and my HRT regimen.

"Well, I transitioned about two years ago and have been on hormones for the same period of time," I said.

"Well you look great for the transition time. What can I do for you?"

"Thank you. I would like to have your advice on different procedures. The first is facial feminization surgery."

As at Dr. Gen's office, Dr. Green's head nurse took my photo from five angles while the doctor looked at me. I joked about feeling like a movie star, and we all laughed as she put the camera's memory card into the computer.

"Okay," Dr. Green said after studying the images for a minute. "On the bottom part of the face I would do nothing. You already have a very nice, feminine face. The forehead is not really very masculine; I have seen women with more of an uplifted forehead than you. For beauty what you can do is the eyelids and your nose, and some time later a hairline transplant. The rest can be done with Botox and some fillers."

"Oh, that sounds like a nice cocktail. I think I agree with the eyelids, considering that my top eyelids are drooping. As far as the nose is concerned, wouldn't I lose some of my facial character?" I asked.

"Yes, you are absolutely right, but it's up to you to know what you want to look like," he said.

"At the moment I will pass on facial surgery, but I would like to ask you about two other things, a tummy tuck and an orchiectomy. Do you do them and what do you propose?"

"Okay, let me see your belly." Dr. Green turned to Victoria. "I hope you are okay that your mother is somewhat naked," he said.

"Oh sure, no issue. I am learning a lot. I've never been to a plastic surgeon before," said Victoria as I got undressed.

"Okay, I see what you mean about the tummy tuck," Dr. Green said. "This is really recommended for you. You have lost weight, and this would make your figure more feminine. You could get your breasts done as well, but this is up to you if you want to have implants or not. As far as the orchiectomy is concerned, I have a very important question: Are you intending to get SRS later?"

"What's SRS?" asked Victoria.

"SRS,[ix] or sex reassignment surgery, is an intervention that changes your sexual organs, meaning it transforms a penis into a vagina," said Dr. Green.

"Wow, I didn't know you could do that," said Victoria.

Dr. Green gave her a smile and then turned to me. "Yes, but my question is if you intend to get SRS after the orchiectomy. If so, we have to take some precautions during the first surgery, meaning we have to open the scrotum lengthwise in the center instead of sideways, which is generally done, because you do not want to have any scars there for the SRS."

"Well, I am in a relationship and I am not thinking about SRS at the moment, but I would not dismiss it entirely," I said. "I would ask you to do the special procedure. As far as the breasts are concerned, I will have to think about it. Is it possible to have three procedures done at the same time?"

"There should be no issue, as they do not touch each other." He turned to his nurse. "Jennifer, any questions? You know what to do?"

"All clear, Dr. Green," she said as I got dressed again. "Manuela, Victoria, please come to the lobby again, and I will get the costs of your interventions together."

"Thank you, Dr. Green," I said before he left. I was grateful to Dr. Green as we followed Jennifer down the hall. I really appreciated his honesty where my face was concerned. Most people I saw tried to sell me all possible surgeries that I don't think I need.

Jennifer presented me with a quote for all the procedures, and after some weeks, I decided to go ahead with the tummy tuck and the orchiectomy. A date for the intervention was set and arranged. First, I had to do some pre-op tests, to make sure all was okay, then book hotels and a surgery room.

Finally, the day came time to go under the knife. I was nervous but happy. I arrived at the ambulant surgery center very early and was prepped for the two operations. I went under the anesthesia and woke up later the same day, when I was transferred to the hotel where I would recuperate for a couple of days before going back home. Approximately two weeks later, I would get the catheter for drainage from the tummy tuck removed. Karen was a big help, she was there to support and help me most of the time during and after the procedure.

One day I was asked about my experiences with these surgeries and said, "I really trusted Dr. Green. He did great work on both surgeries. The only issue was having to travel every time for four hours to see him, and well, there is pain, a lot of pain. Again, you really have to want to do this."

One year later I had the other two surgeries, breast augmentation and eyelid surgery. This time, because these were more common procedures that weren't transgender-specific, I did them with a doctor who was only a half-hour drive from her house.

While looking for a surgeon I had interviews with about five doctors, all with different propositions and price levels. Only two understood that I was a transgender woman. In the end I chose a doctor that had already done the breasts of three of my friends. It was a recommendation and a very good one. He was very informative before the surgery, which gave me a lot of confidence about the outcome.

The eyelid surgery was something that I needed, since they were very heavy. This was not necessarily a feminization surgery, but something that I would have to do in any case.

Breast augmentation surgery[x] is a special operation; it is certainly not as complicated as other surgeries but is something that has to be done properly. For transgender it is not as it is for cis woman. Some of the main questions we get are the size of the implants, if our skin can support such an implant without cracking, and the position of incision because of the scar. For transgender women the choices are not so vast, even though one's choice of surgeon is critical to success.

Another factor to take into account is the time on hormones and the size of breasts you've already achieved before getting your breast augmentation. I had already had two years on hormones and was already a B to a C cup, so the needed implants were relatively small to get to a D cup. Many specialists say that one needs two to three years on hormones to arrive at a stable level of feminization, meaning breast size, skin type, and all factors, but this also depends on the level of hormones taken. All people react differently, so heredity is a factor as well. Some doctors say a trans woman will get approximately half the size of her mother's or sisters' breasts before they had children.

In all respects, as far as surgical interventions are concerned, transgender people, both women and men, should look for experience and professionality from a surgeon. There have been many unfortunate cases, many that I've heard of in South Florida, that prove that a lot of care and good research are important first steps.

Paperwork

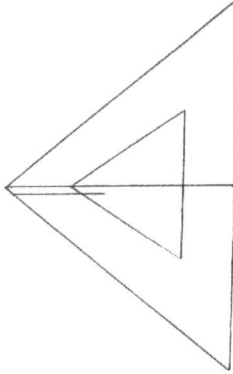

"Every person's true identity is beautiful, and much of the
ugliness we observe in others was put inside of them by
external influences."
Bryant McGill

Good looks, perfect behavior, and speech patterns
that match up with your real gender are
unfortunately not enough to live life as transgender
people wish to do so. Paperwork can also be a real
issue. For instance, if you've been transitioning and
a policeman does not recognize you in the picture
on your driver's license, there can be some issues
coming. The gender marked there and the
difference in name can be killers for transgender
people.

Coming Home to Venus

In some Bible Belt states in the US and in many countries around the world, the degree of discrimination against transgender people is very high and they are not protected by law. Imagine the following scenario. This was true for some time in the US and, chillingly, could become so again.

June was driving from New York back home to Florida after quite a lot of work with the company she had just started working for. She was driving down I-95, the interstate highway that starts at the Canadian border and ends in Miami, a long, long way. She was getting tired; she had had the morning with her new bosses finishing the training that was expected from her, and then drove over nine hours. During the trip, June was thinking, 'I am so happy this company does not mind that I am transgender, though they did ask me to get my papers updated urgently, and that is going to be my first priority when I get back to Florida." June was a very passable transgender woman. She was thin, sexy, very feminine in both voice and manners; there was no reason for someone to misgender her.

'It's time to stop for the night and get something to eat,' she thought. 'My trip is almost over now." She scrolled through her phone's map for a suitable hotel. 'Ten Miles to the next hotel, and it is not such a bad one, I think. Let's go there.' She followed the directions and entered this brand-new hotel belonging to a large chain in a small town called Selma, North Carolina. She entered the hotel and approached the check-in desk where an older woman was working.

She asked for a room for the evening and was given some good options for a good rate.

"Okay, please give me your ID and credit card so that I can book it for you," said the attendant. June handed them both to her. The attendant looked at them, then looked at June, and said, "Sorry, madam, I need your ID."

"Oh, I see. I am a transgender woman, and I have not changed my papers yet. They are still under my old name and gender."

"The attendant frowned., I see. Michael, in this state we are not allowed to receive transgender people. You cannot stay here. Please leave our premises."

June was completely shocked and felt very hurt and horrible, but she walked back to her car. In Florida she'd never such an experience; it felt degrading. "How can I find another hotel?"

She drove to a nearby hotel and called them from the parking lot.

Coming Home to Venus

"Good evening, how can I help you?" was the answer on the other end.

"Hi, my name is June. Do you have available rooms?"

"Yes, ma'am, we do," said the man on the other end of the line.

"Perfect. I am a transgender woman, I am coming to your hotel. I will be there in five minutes."

"Sorry, Madam, our state does not accept transgender people in our hotels," said the man and he hung up.

'Shit, shit, shit,' thought June, 'what am I going to do? I am too tired to drive farther. Plus I doubt it's any better in South Carolina, and on top of that I have another ten hours' drive to get home. There is only one thing I can do: sleep in the car and drive farther tomorrow morning.'

June went to a small restaurant, ate some food, and found a place near a hotel where there were other cars so she would not be so exposed. It was kind of weird sleeping in the car. Fortunately it was summer, and the temperature was not an issue. She managed to pass the night more or less okay. In the morning she took the car and drove it to a nearby gas station to go to the bathroom and get some food. She took her toiletry things out of the bag for minimum hygiene. She still had some facial hair, what most probably gave a reason for people to understand that she was a transgender, so a good shave was needed. She entered the gas station shop and went directly to the woman's restroom, closed the door of her cubical, and did what she had to do. All of a sudden, she heard the voices of people coming to the bathroom. It was very strange.

"Sir, this is a women's bathroom. Please leave immediately," said one of the voices.

"What, can't I piss in peace?" said June.

"Please come out immediately!" said the voice.

June adjusted her skirt and opened the door; it was a policeman. "You are under arrest for being in a women's toilet. It is banned for men to go to women's toilets. Please follow me and give me your papers." The policeman escorted her out of the toilet to her car, where she gave him the papers. Then he put her in handcuffs and drove her to the station. Though she stayed in prison for only a couple of days and left on bail, of course she stayed with the men and was raped multiple times by the inmates.

Although this is just a fictional story, it had been a reality for some time here in the US. Transgender people still use a safe, transgender map[xi] of the US, where states are considered dangerous. Well most states have laws discriminating LGBT and transgender people, as a matter of fact a large part of the Midwest and bible belt.

In some other countries it is similar or even worse. I know a girl in an Arabic country, a very beautiful, fully passable transgender girl, that gets beaten and raped by the local police for being transgender. In most Arabic countries it is not possible to change one's papers, so being caught is putting your life at risk.

With what is going on around the world as far as discrimination is concerned many transgender people have decided to live stealthily so that they will not have many issues. But even for that you need the right papers, and that is not always easy.

And to get the right papers is not easy; it can be a real jungle. There are no uniform laws in the US or elsewhere in the world regarding this matter; everybody has different codes to follow.

In the first case are the countries or regions with no transgender recognition—in other words, no possibility of changing your legal documents. This includes much of Africa and the Middle East, Central America and some US states.

The second case is countries or regions where it is possible to change your gender ID but proof of bottom surgery is required. This includes a large part of US, including Florida, as well as some European and Asian countries.

The third case is that one can change their gender ID on their paperwork with letters from psychiatric specialists without the need for surgery or hormonal change. Parts of the US, South America, and parts of Europe and Asia are like that.

The most important paper to change is of course your birth certificate. If you can change this paper, then you can change all of your methods of identification, but not all transgender people can do it. It is possible in the US to have a driver's license and even a social security card as a woman but still have a birth certificate lying and calling you male.

My case may have been even more complicated due to my multiple nationalities. I was born in Portugal, have a dual citizenship with Switzerland, and live in the US. Luckily I was born in Portugal where the third case applies, meaning I was able to change my gender identity by presenting the government with psychiatric papers to that effect. So the natural way for me to go was to change my birth certificate in Portugal and then change all the other papers in Switzerland and the US. This is by no means a norm but a choice; in the US you can change your name and gender data by court order, then change all your IDs without changing your birth certificate. This is of course only valid for American citizens, which is why I did what I did, since I travel a lot for business.

Most information about changing your gender identity on your paperwork can be found online. I started with the different transgender associations of different countries. For the US this is Transequality;[xii] for Switzerland, the Transgender Network Switzerland;[xiii] and for Portugal I could not find any, so I had to go to the Portuguese consulate in Palm Coast, Florida. I was dressed at the time as man, with very long hair, which looked kind of funny.

"Hi," I said in Portuguese to the lady at the counter of the consulate. "My name is Fernando. I have an appointment for my passport and my ID renewal."

"Hi, Fernando. Please sit down and wait. We will call you in a second," said the lady.

"I have a question," I added, trying to get all her courage together. "I found this documentation concerning transgender name and gender changes on a person's birth certificate and papers. Can you help me to apply for it?"

"Okay, let me look at the documents," said the lady with a distressed look on her face. "I have never seen anything like this before, so let me ask our consul. Probably he has better information than I do." She left for the room behind the counter in apparent shock.

I sat down and comforted myself with the fact that I knew this was going to take some time. After ten minutes and about five people looking at me to see who had asked, the woman came back and said, "Please come in through the door, I will open it."

I stood up, the door opened, and I entered the inside of the consulate. The lady led me to an office and asked me to sit down. It was surely the consul's office, with the Portuguese coat of arms and a portrait of the Portuguese president hanging on the wall.

About five minutes later, a gentleman came and sat behind the large desk. He presented himself as Don Alfonso, the Portuguese consul for Florida.

"I have to be honest," he said. "We have never seen such a case for name and gender change on the ID and birth certificate. From the papers that you produced I can see it's a new law. It started last year, and you have to apply directly to the central registers in Lisbon. Our role will be only to certify all papers, that means the translations."

"Oh, okay," I said. "Do you think it will be a fast process? And do I send the papers directly to the central registers or will you do it, since you are my representative here in the US?"

"I have no Idea about how long it will take. As I told you we have no experience with such documents, and the central registers are not the fastest institution in the world. I sent my divorce papers six months ago and am still waiting, and I deal with them on a daily basis. I would recommend you have a representative in Lisbon that can follow the case, usually a lawyer."

"Oh, that is a great idea. We have a family lawyer in Portugal; she can take care of this," I said.

"But don't be surprised if she has no experience with such procedure; as I said, it is a very new one," said Don Alfonso, looking at the list of requirements I brought him. "You need a petition letter and two letters from psychiatrists as well as copies of their diplomas and proof that they are transgender specialists."

"Yes, I will ask my counselors for the letters. They are very similar to the WPATH letters that are made here in the US."

"Okay. Then you have to have everything translated by an official translator. I can give you the contact information for Ana Maria. She is someone we use a lot and she can use our stamp, so I will only have to sign them before you send them to the lawyer."

"Oh, thank you, you are very supportive."

"Our pleasure, but next time come the way you are comfortable." He smiled gently. "We have no judgments here, and we are very supportive. "

"Oh, thank you," I said again. "I never expected this."

"Another thing: what is the name you are asking for?"

"I would like my name to be changed to Florence Manuela Marques," I said. "I want to maintain my initials."

"Um, that will not work. Florence is not a Portuguese name, and the central registers will only let you have Portuguese names. Why don't you use the Portuguese name for Florence? Flora? It is the name of the wife of Eusébio, and she is very cute," said Don Alfonso. Eusébio was one of the best football players that Portugal ever produced, a national hero and a keen talent. Flora was a very beautiful multiracial woman, and very famous as well.

"I think that this is a very good idea. I will have to rethink, but you just gave me great advice."

"No problem. That is what we are here for. Please come with me. We are going to get all your photos and things done for your passport and ID card."

I took Flora Manuela as my new official name, then visited Dr. Carol Clark and Dr. Jamie Weiss, two recognized specialists is transgender care, to get the necessary letters and their CVs. It took some weeks until all of it was done; then I sent all the papers to Ana Maria for translation.

Ana Maria made the translation, and I made an appointment at the consulate for the notarial signature. That morning I drove from Boca Raton to Flagler Beach, where I met Ana Maria.

I opened the door of the little office and said, "Hi? Anybody here?"

"Of course! Here I am," said Ana Maria, who was sitting behind a desk in the corner of the office. "You are Manuela? Come here, I have all the papers ready for you."

"Oh, thank you, here you are."

"Sit down, Manuela, or should I say Flora? Do you have five minutes? I would love to exchange some words with you," she said. "I want to tell you that I really admire your courage. I find you an incredible woman. You look really nice, and you are fighting to be yourself."

"Oh, thank you. You are too kind. I am just trying to be myself, who I feel I am." I was feeling really happy to hear someone that understood what I was going through.

"I have a friend here in Flagler Beach that is transgender, but she has having a lot of problems. She is too scared and not being accepted, so I think you are an incredible person. The letters from your psychiatrists are very clear about you. It made for interesting translation work. But what are you going to do with them? Please tell me."

"I am going to send them to the central registers in Lisbon and ask them to change my name and gender on my birth certificate. I am a woman, and I want my birth certificate to show that."

"Oh, I didn't know you could do that in Portugal."

"Yes, there is a new law, and apparently until now only twelve people have applied for a name and gender change. We will see what happens."

Ana Maria and I exchanged some words about Portugal, where we came from and how long we'd been in the US, and then I drove another half hour to the consulate for the notarial signature.

After ten minutes of waiting, Don Alfonso greeted me in the lobby. "Hi, Flora," he said. "Nice to see you again. I am so happy that you took my advice with your name. Here you have your papers signed as needed. Please let me have the honor of making you the new passport and ID cards, after the changes."

"Oh, thank you, Don Alfonso," I said.

"I hope that it all goes well and quickly. Apart from that, how are you doing?"

"I am doing great; all is changing and progressing in a very positive way. Thank you for asking."

I went back home, sent all the papers to my lawyer in Lisbon, and it did take about six months and a lot of money to get the process approved. One paper was demanded, and that was an official acceptance from my wife of a same-sex marriage.

One day a letter came with my new birth certificate. Under name, it said, "Flora Manuela Marques," and under gender "female." Wow, that brought a lot of very good emotions to me. Again, I went to the consulate, this time for my new passport and ID under my new name and gender.

The next order of business was my Swiss nationality and to get my papers updated in the US. For Switzerland I asked the advice of the Transgender Association, and got in contact with the Swiss consulate, sending them the new birth certificate. It took another six months of going through the Swiss consulate in Portugal and until I got it all certified.

Switzerland is still one of those countries where a confirmation of reassignment surgery is requested, but since I was born in Portugal and my birth certificate was changed, they had to accept it. It took many telephone calls and many emails to make sure that things were progressing. All went through, and one day, about six months later, I was invited to go to Atlanta to get my new Swiss passport and ID. In the end, Switzerland was very efficient; one could get everything done by phone and email, only the ID and passport had to be done in the consulate. The Swiss and Portuguese systems are very similar; they have this machine where your photograph is taken along with your fingerprints and all the information is wired directly to a central system. Then the passport and ID are made directly and shipped from the central office to the consulate and then to the person in question.

The only place left to update my papers was the US. Well, if Portugal and Switzerland love efficiency, the US inherited a love of something else from their past colonizers, Britain, and that is called bureaucracy. The love for forms and documents in this country is insatiable.

The first thing I had to do was get my green card, or legal residence status, updated. I went to the local immigration office and waited until my number came up to see one of the clerks. This was done later, after my divorce.

"Hi, my name is Flora Marques. I just had a name and gender change, and I would like to update my green card. I have here some papers, my new birth certificate, and my passport. What else do you need?" I asked.

"Let me have your green card and all the papers," said the clerk. She started to study all the papers. After some minutes she asked to see my court order.

"I do not have a court order," I explained. "In Portugal where I was born, it is not required."

"Just a moment," said the clerk, and she disappeared with all my documents. I waited a good half hour until she came back, this time with another person, her supervisor.

"Okay," the supervisor said. "This is not easy, but please bring official translations of your birth certificate. We are opening a new process for you, so you have to get your fingerprints taken and you will receive an invitation by mail. We are keeping your green card here and stamping your passport in case you travel abroad. Can you confirm your address please?"

"Yes, I confirm the address," I said. "And by the way at the same time I would like to confirm my divorce. Here is a copy of the court decision." And she gave the paper to one of the clerks

"Oh, this is good. It should help your first request because you have both your previous name and present name listed, and it's signed by a court. We will inform you about the dates for your appointment."

Very soon I got my invitation to be fingerprinted, and soon after I got my renewed green card. Unfortunately in the US there is no one-stop shop for all documents and administrative matters, so my next stop was the Social Security Administration.

I thought at this time that nothing could stop me. I looked online, where it was clear that you could change your name and gender for the Social Security Administration based on your birth certificate and green card, so I decided to go to the nearest Social Security office to get it done. As usual, I arrived with all my paperwork, took a number, and waited for my turn. Then my number was called and I went to the clerk.

"Hi, I would like to update my records with my name and gender change as well as with my divorce. Here are all the documents," I said to the clerk and gave her all the papers.

She asked for my social security card, so I handed it to her and she entered all the information in the computer. I could see that the clerk was having some sort of problems, so I said, "Here is my birth certificate with translation, and here is my new green card, my passport, and the certificate of my divorce."

"I can see," said the clerk, not in a very friendly manner. She stood up and went to the back of the office. I waited about one hour; then she came back with another lady and said, "Do you have a court confirmation?"

"No, in Portugal where I come from it is not needed, and on your website it stated that if you have a birth certificate it is enough. Immigration accepted it like this as well."

"Well we do not know what the other departments do. For Social Security you need a court confirmation; otherwise we cannot change anything. Go and get one, and then we will make your changes," said the second woman at the same time that she handed my papers back.

I was really upset. I had spent a lot of time working on this, and though I'd made good headway, this setback felt like I had no results. I phoned a friend, Morgan; he and his wife, Ashley, are champions for the transgender community in South Florida. They have an organization that supports and helps many of the community.

"Hi Morgan, how are you?" I said.

We exchanged pleasantries and then I said, "Morgan, I went to the Social Security Office today to change my name and gender, and presented all the papers. I already have my birth certificate changes, my green card and all, but they are requesting a court confirmation of my name change. I don't have one, since it was not necessary for my birth certificate in Portugal. I don't understand why they are demanding this."

"No problem. Which office did go to?"

"The one in Boca Raton in Palm Beach."

"That explains everything. Once you have the court papers, they will find another issue. We know them; they are not transgender-friendly, so they always have an issue," said Morgan. "No, we have to make an official complaint and go to another office."

"Oh, but I thought the law was the same for everyone," I said.

"Yes, the law is the same, but the interpretation is not. I will be in the office in Pembroke Pines next Wednesday with another transgender person. Join us and let's see how it goes."

"I thought I had to go to the one Palm Beach County because that's where I live."

"Not really. They are federal offices, so you can go wherever you want," he said.

"Okay, perfect. Thanks a lot, let me know where it is and what time we should meet."

Morgan sent all of the information to me, and we met at the parking of the right Social Security Office the following Wednesday.

"Ella, come with us, let's get this done," said Morgan. We all went in, got numbers, and waited our turns, talking and having fun. Finally, my turn came, and we went to see the clerk. We sat in front of the window, and Morgan started. "Hi, I am here to support Flora. She will tell you everything."

"I would like to update my file," I said. "I changed my birth certificate in Portugal, updated my name and gender marker, changed my green card, and am now doing it with you guys so that I can have my ID updated. Please find enclosed all documents."

"Okay, let's start with your social security card," said the clerk.

"Here it is," I said, "and the translation of the birth certificate, the passport, and the green card."

"Please give me the original birth certificate in Portuguese; that is always better," said the clerk and they filled all the information in on the computer. "Okay, I have all that is as required. you will receive your new Social Security card by mail; for your new driving license, please wait two days so that everything is updated correctly."

"Oh, thank you! Is that all?" I asked. It was startlingly easy after the time I had in Palm Beach.

"Sure, no problem."

I did not have any issues getting my driver's license changed, not to mention much later my nationality as an American citizen, so all of my paperwork was finished in about two years' time.

Coming Home to Venus

As usual, with many parts of the transgender experience, patience and perseverance are the most important things. It also helps to have good friends and resources like Morgan and Don Alfonso to help when we get discouraged.

Of course, during my transition, not everything went as smoothly.

Coming Home to Venus

Breaking the Ties

"To fight and conquer in all our battles is not supreme
excellence; supreme excellence consists in breaking the
enemy's resistance without fighting."

Sun Tzu

"Hi, everybody, how are you all doing? Glad you
made it for this transgender support group," said
Jan, the host of the Lake Worth group. There were
about twenty different people in attendance and
only two were cis. After the usual introductions and
statements concerning the rules of the meeting, Jan
said, "Who wants to start?"

I was eager to speak because I had something big on
my mind. I stood up and said, "Hi, everybody, I
would like to talk about family ties when you
transition. What are your expectations and

experiences? In most respects I have been blessed; my family has been very supportive. My sisters, my children, and in the beginning of my transition even my ex-wife was a great support. She knew about my tendencies and little escapades for a long time, actually since I met her, over twenty-five years ago. All went well for a long time, so I expected to be able to transition and still have a stable relationship. Well, things deteriorated, not only because I was a changing but also because her expectations grew away from the nest. The details are very tough, and the last six months of our marriage were devastating. But this is somehow a common fact of life for us. Many marriages break down, and with transitioning things can get worse. I just thought for a while that we would be an exception."

"Well, there are exceptions," said Rachel. "Some marriages will still persist, mainly with older couples. I have seen as many couples stay together, mainly if they have been together for a long time and there is a high degree of mutual trust. On the other hand I have seen many transgender people decide not to make a complete transition and live a crossdresser's life in parallel to their marriage. In my case, I was already divorced before I decided to transition, so there were no real issues."

"We are all different, but it is true that many of us have similar experiences, and that is for both trans men and trans women," Jan said. "Many marriages or relationships break during transitions, and there are many factors that have to be taken into consideration. There are many changes, not only in the way a transgender person looks but also in their behavior and feelings. Never underestimate the effect of hormones on the body changes, but also on behavior. This is one point that is not always acceptable for the partners of transgender people, and it is difficult for both parties involved. I have seen many lesbian couples in which one transitions to become a man, and the acceptance from the woman is really not there anymore. Sometimes the effect of hormones on a trans man can be very distressing for the partner—not only the hair growth but also the moods are very intense.

"It is not only an issue with partners but with family members as well," she mused. "Children of transgender people sometimes put their backs to their parents because they are ashamed of them; parents refuse to accept or understand their trans kids... yes, there are many ties that can be broken during transition."

"I am the living proof of what you just said," said June. "My parents are evangelical Christians and very religious; they have known that I was transgender since I was very young, but they always fought my feelings, refusing to accept me. I am thirty-one now and transitioned ten years ago. My youth was very difficult. I was constantly being hurt and punished because I was not man enough in their eyes, and the fact that I wore sometimes girls' clothes in hiding was taken as the work of the devil. So I did everything to go out of the house and create my own life. As soon as I was old enough to take care of myself, I transitioned; I had some friends help me, and I did not see my parents for a long time. About two years ago I approached them to tell them that I was still alive and I missed them. They misgendered me, they still do, and they treated me like I was the devil, like I was the worst person in the world. It really bothers me, so I decided to ignore them again. I cannot live with their negativity and the way they treat me."

"Well, luckily there are people that have compassion and understanding, like our two parents here," said Jan.

"Yes, indeed," said Jane, one of the two cis people there. "Dexter and I wanted to know what it means to be transgender as soon as Patrick, our son that was born a girl, told us. We immediately attended a support group in order to better understand transgender people, and we are so glad we did. We found people that are quite amazing, and who understand what Patrick was going through. We have been attending support groups for almost two years now, and we are even thinking of starting our own group. We have heard so many times about family members, meaning parents, siblings, children, and of course partners, being aggressive and difficult with transgender people, giving them no acceptance, especially if the families are very religious. I always thought that religion was to do with compassion and mutual help, but some religions do exactly the opposite. But the lack of acceptance by society is very large and not always easy to understand. After all being transgender is not a choice; it's the way you are born."

"Yes, you are all so right," I said. "My partner and I were married for a very long time and we grew together very much as a couple. We had a very nice life together. Although I am sure that being transgender was part of the reason why we divorced, it was certainly not the only one. There were other issues we went through, and let's face it, fifty percent of all couples divorce. It is normal. Life is a journey, a marriage is a common journey, and sometimes there are curves and changes along the way."

Coming Home to Venus

"We divorced some three years ago at the beginning of my transition. We were married only for three years. We had no children and she told me that she could not live with this, she was not a lesbian, and so she left the house. I suffered a lot, but it didn't stop me from transitioning. I carried on, but I went into depression and I was feeling really bad. I then had the choice of being myself or falling for her and denying it like most people do. Well, I decided to fight for what I felt was right and be myself and carried on with my journey without her. Two years later she came back trying to get together again with me. That could not happen. I decided that if she had let me down before, she would do it again, and I could not have coped with it." Said another girl

"I'm having the same issue right now," said another girl in the group. I have two small children, and my wife is making a lot of pressure for me to stop. She told me that she will leave if I carry on wearing woman's clothes. I honestly do not know what to do. I am getting depressed, I even thought about killing myself. My feelings won't go away. Why is she so selfish? We could discuss if I will do a complete transition or if I will cross-dress from time to time, but this is part of me. I cannot live without it."

"Wow, that sounds extremely difficult," said Jan. "Please do not commit suicide. I think it's better to have an ex-partner or an estranged parent of a child that is alive and transgender than a dead person that refused to find him or herself."

"I think that she would prefer me to be dead than to be a transgender woman," said the woman.

"We hope that is not the case. Have you tried to go to a marriage counselor? Someone that could help you both?" asked Jan.

"Yes, we are thinking about it. It is an issue, but we are fighting from both sides. Probably we will get to a compromise."

"After my divorce I had quite a lot of different thoughts about the whole thing, and I came up with some important points to rule my life. Points that I hope will stay with me forever," I said. "The first is that I am responsible for my life; nobody will or can run it for me. I cannot give happiness to others if I cannot be happy myself, and I have to be in charge of this. In a partnership both partners have to be happy for everything to function correctly."

"Yes, that is very profound and true," said Jan.

"If I might add, my other lesson is that, as a transgender woman, I tried all my life to run away from my feelings and please the rest of civilization, not myself. I just wanted to show what I didn't have, happiness. Probably I was trying to please my mother all this time, which is why I married a woman who had strong similarities to her. I believe that the marriage did not work because, all of a sudden, I started to be happy, changing the course of the marriage, and the other partner felt deprived and not happy anymore. And this leads to another lesson that I have learned: don't let yourself be manipulated by others. Follow your own feelings, and don't listen to people that are too selfish. They only see what is good for them. A marriage is by definition a compromise between two parties. But a good compromise has to be based on a win-win situation for both parties. That implies that both are happy and both respect each other. Manipulation and a lack of self-respect are the enemy of happiness in a couple—that is, unless you are in a sadomasochistic relationship, I honestly tried to find compromises to actively ensure my partner was happy, but if everything is broken, it does not work anymore."

"Yes, but then you have to find help, someone outside the marriage that gives you advice and tries to help the couple," said Jan.

"Yes, we tried, but I believe it was too late for us," I said.

"I had a very similar situation in my marriage," said Rach. "We went to a marriage counselor, and it got very manipulative and negative. It got to the point that either I would renounce my transition or she would leave me. I said I would rather be dead, but she didn't care anymore. Until then I thought that I knew her, then I found out that I didn't. She became a monster, cold and completely selfish."

"Yes, I think you are right. You only know someone when such things happen and the person you thought you knew transforms into something completely different," I said. "And in that moment you cannot be impressed by the harassment and negativity that is coming at you. You have to stay in control, be in charge of yourself and your own feelings. For a trans woman, anyway, losing control can be a big issue. I have heard stories of wives calling the police in such tense moments, and of course the trans woman is mostly portrayed as guilty in the eyes of the law. We still have too many enemies, or at least people that think that transgender people are guilty of everything. I remember during the stressful periods while we were really fighting and we lived in the same house that every time we had a fight, or there was a conflict brewing, I would retire to my part of the house and lock it for protection."

"The issue of home violence for transgender people is not easy. I have heard of many such cases; especially for people that are under the influence of alcohol or drugs it can be very critical," said Jan. "In many cases transgender women land in male jails, and that is another big, big issue. In some counties they land in solitary confinement but not everywhere."

"In any case I have only one piece of advice: do everything possible to increase your self-confidence and embrace the unknown," I concluded. "Be positive and attract positivity in everything you do. The more you get into negative feelings the worse you will get until you cannot get out of it. But in all divorces, this is the case. If you are transgender or not it's a detail, not to our advantage, but still a detail. There are always challenging times—after the divorce as well. Both marriage and divorce are for life, meaning you will always be involved somehow with the other person, and in a divorce you behind many things that you did together. Kids will be an eternal remembrance of your partner somehow. I do not regret the twenty-five years we spent together. It was a great time, I certainly put everything into question during the last six months of the marriage and when we were filling for divorce, but I believe both my ex and I have somehow healed and started our own lives and journeys, which is so important for our mental health. I have no animosity anymore when I see her or think of her."

"Breaking ties is always difficult to say the least, and with your kids it's very sad indeed," said a woman named Michaela. "I never talked that much to my two sons, but since my transition, they refuse to talk to me. I have written them letters, they do not answer; I phone them and they do not take the call. It is very distressing. I want to tell them how much I love them and to express my sorrows for those times that I was so nervous that I did not have time for them, but their mother told me that they were ashamed that a trans woman was their father. They cannot understand my choice, if only being transgender was a choice, but they do not know any better."

"Yes, Michaela, many of us have that destiny," said Jan. "I think we should wrap up for this evening. If there are no more comments, I'll see you all next week."

The meeting was over and most of the people that attended that meeting went out to dinner, where of course more comments and experiences were shared.

Coming Home to Venus

As I drove home, I thought, 'God, pardon my ex for the pain she induced in me. Those six months of pain will stay in my memory forever. No, it was a time of learning; one can say that you only know someone really well when you have seen the good and the bad sides. Love closes the eyes and makes emotions rosy and beautiful; fighting is the opposite. It brings your defense mechanisms to foreground and you are ready to hurt in order to defend yourself. When you experience both with the same person, the extremes arise.

'I just hope that the pain that I caused her was less than the pain she gave me, though I have no doubt that the pain was mutual. The details are sometimes so painful; selfishness, aggression, manipulation were some of the adjectives that I can only remember. They led to stabbing, hurting feelings, and I am sure it went both ways. I know it is very common in such situations. When you're going through a divorce, you are trying to defend yourself and your livelihood. My first divorce was not at all like that; we had a mutual understanding that we had to change our lives and we found a solution that was okay for us both, without too much aggression and trying to hurt the other just for the fun of it. Well, let bygones be bygones. It is important to recover, to get strong again and concentrate on the healing process. Any time of change is a time of reflection; in a divorce the change is massive and the directions of one's life take a big, big turn.'

That divorce period really left its marks on me. In the beginning we both tried, somehow, to save the marriage. We went to a marriage counselor to discuss the issues, but it was clear that there was no return and we went to the lawyers instead. We finally reached an agreement, and the marriage was dissolved. But as usual the devil is in the details and that was what hurt. During all this time we were living in the same house, though divided, with the common ground as the kitchen, living room, and gardens, so there was a continuous, common presence that increased the negativity.

The house was sold after the divorce, and each of us went in a different direction. For me it was a time of healing and a time to increase my self-confidence. I was a very lucky girl; I survived the moment without major issues, which is not the case of so many transgender people. In difficult moments many transgender people become homeless, survive through sex work, start with drugs and alcohol, or even die by suicide. When you think about breaking the ties, you have to think about the transgender kids whose parents tell them to leave the house and never come back again. This is still a reality; the lack of societal understanding is immense when it comes to transgender people.

According to the National Center for Transgender equality, [xiv] 57 percent of transgender people faced rejection from their own families. Forty-five percent of transgender people ended their relationships after coming out, and this number boosts to 73 percent for those over the age of fifty-five. With dissolutions of marriages, 29 percent of transgender people experienced the limiting of contact with their children by ex-partners. Nineteen percent reported home violence by family members because they were transgender or gender non-conforming. Sixty-one percent of transgender children experience harassment.

These are sad statistics in this day and age, but unfortunately the outlook in many parts of the world at the moment has a tendency to be worse, not better. In the US between January 2017 and February 2020, the Trump administration introduced sixty-seven pieces of legislation limiting LGBTQ and transgender rights, according to the list by the NCTE.[xv] In the last few years, for a reason unknown to me, there has been a global movement that is very anti-LGBTQ, especially against the community's weakest link, transgender people. We hope that this trend changes. We are experiencing a split of many churches because of this theme, LGBTQ rights. Transgender people are just people; we are a small part of the population, but it is a global phenomenon that has existed since the beginning of the world, so why is there continuous persecution against transgender people? It is understandable that in the case of a couple there are major sexual and compatibility issues with transitioning, but at a social level, it is not understandable.

As I got home from support group that night, I had another thought.

Wow. I survived.

I am alive, living as my real self and trying to find myself, my environment, and my femininity. I believe that the time in life when you transition is so crucial. The later you transition, the more ties you may lose, but it is not necessarily sad that that is the case.

I have to give a huge compliment to the parents of transgender people that accept and help their children. Yes, an emphatic yes, it's better to see them transitioning than to see them dead. In all these years I have seen so many fantastic parents that come to our meetings to grow, to learn what is coming to them and their kids. Sure, the idea of having a transgender kid comes with the idea of how safety and security for their kids changes, but thank God, times have changed. There is a considerably larger acceptance of transgender people now than compared to ten or twenty years ago.

May this progress continue.

Coming Home to Venus

New Life, New Beginning

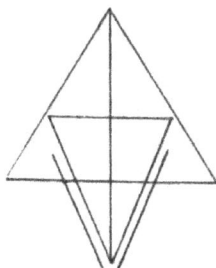

"Rather than turning the page, it's much easier to just throw
the book away."
Anthony Liccione

Now I was divorced, I had found a new place to live.
Now it was time to be myself and start a new life. As
a matter of fact I had gone through a tremendous
change not only in my private life but also in my
business, because one of the companies I was
working with was sold and I lost the contract to
work with them.

With my new life, new people appeared. It is true
that many were from the transgender community,
though others were cis people. The divorce and the
changes in the business brought a lot of worries and
uncertainties, so I tried to look for job where I could
still have and continue my own business. I found a

job selling insurance, which was not really the most interesting job in the world, but it gave me the opportunity to have strong business exposure as a woman for the first time.

On a Monday morning, I started my new job in the insurance industry.

"So, it says here in the application 'Fernando.' Is that you?" asked Tom, my new supervisor.

"Yes, my chosen name is Manuela but my papers are not completely processed, so my ID is still under Fernando."

"Okay, that is not an issue. We can put all your documents under your chosen name, but your contract has to be done under your legal name," he said.

I filled out my onboarding paperwork, then went to the conference room where there were a lot of people waiting for the Monday meeting to start. Some were apparently new like me.

"Hi, Manuela," a man said as he walked up. "I'm Rob. I am going to be your mentor during your training, so let's make sure you listen to me properly."

"Hi, Rob, okay, I see you have a great opinion about my listening," I said with a smile.

"So where do you come from? I notice an accent."

"I am Swiss and Portuguese," I said. "I speak seven languages."

"That is great. Around here we need mostly Spanish and French—apart from English of course."

"And where do you come from?" I asked. "I mean you do have a heavy Spanish accent."

"I come from Venezuela, but have been living here for fifteen years."

"Hi, everybody, let's start this meeting," Tom shouted and some thirty five people that were there started to move towards him to hear better. "As usual, I will start by welcoming the new members, then discuss the sales figures and prizes for last week. I would like to start by welcoming Manuela Marques; she is a Swiss-Portuguese girl and she knows seven languages, so she really can help with the enrollments when there are non English speaking people."

As he said that everybody clapped, and some greeted me.

Tom carried out that meeting with all the sales values and gave praise to some people, including Rob. I had never seen such a show, with praise and a lot of motivation being given to most of the people who were present. The meeting went on for a good hour; afterward all the people that were under Rob went to a meeting room to make a timetable for the week. During the meeting I was never misgendered or looked at in a funny way. I was really one of the girls. It was a very strange and new experience, but I enjoyed it. I had never been in such a sales motivation meeting before. I had spent all my life in sales, with many hours of sales meetings behind me, but I had never experienced something like that. But I was trying to get some feedback on how people perceived me, and all in all, it increased my self-awareness and self-confidence. I was happy and could feel a lot of respect coming from my coworkers.

Finally the day came that I was going to see some customers. I was sitting in my car, waiting for Rob to appear, and thinking, 'My first customer experience as a girl! Is my hair okay? My makeup? Do I look professional? It's so important to present correctly to customers."

Soon Rob arrived and I caught up with him.

"Wow, girl! You rock, you look great," he said. "I like your earrings; they look really nice. So today we are going to make some door-to-door visits in this area. There are quite a lot of medical companies, doctor's offices, testing companies, and we are going to promote our product here. Since it is your first day you just listen. "

We entered a doctor's office and walked directly to the counter.

"Hi. How are you today?" said Rob with a big smile at the girls behind the desk.

"Very well, thank you for asking. How can I help you?"

"My name is Rob and this is Manuela. I would like to ask you if you are happy with your company's benefits and if we can help you."

"Hi, I am sorry, but we already had your colleagues from LAC visit yesterday. We are very busy now, and yes, we are very happy with our company benefits, so please do not come back," she said, so we headed out.

Rob didn't let this faze him. We walked next door, to the next doctor's office.

"Hi. How are you doing today?" Rob said again with the usual big smile. That was part of his normal prospecting routine.

For two hours we visited a lot of prospects. Most of them were negative; only two set up a meeting. For me, it was a nice opportunity to see a lot of people in a somewhat professional way; not once was I misgendered or looked at in a funny way. By the third day of visits I was doing the talking and Rob was being the support; there again all went very well. With time and training, I was doing it all, including the first interviews with the owners and earning some money.

While I worked for the insurance company, I kept up my own business on the side. Some weeks after my divorce, I received a telephone call from an old friend in India. They has worked together for the same company during over fifteen years.

"Hi, Fernando, how are you doing?" Gian asked.

"Hi, Gian, nice to hear from you. I am doing okay, and you?"

Gian did not know about my transition, and I chose not to tell him at that time.

"I am doing great. All is well with my new company; it is going in a very good direction. I want to ask you if you are interested in representing in the US a company from India that makes coils and bars for generators. It is a family-owned company, very nice people, that wants to start exporting to the US."

"Wow, that sounds very interesting, and comes at a great time since I lost recently a Swiss company from my clients."

"Perfect, I will put you in contact with this company, and R is going to contact you soon."

"Thank you, Gian. I hope to come to see you in India soon."

Well, that was the beginning of something very nice, a new connection. R phoned me, and after some negotiations a contract between both companies was made and I started to represent the Indian company in the US. Our communication was very good, even if we had not seen each other. In the beginning I communicated under the name Fernando, but after some months it changed to Flora Manuela and it has been a great to work together ever since.

I had transitioned in my private life some three years before I transitioned in my business. This was creating some issues. My hair was growing, my voice changing, and I was more and more feminine. It was getting to the point that once a customer called me weird, an increasingly feminine man.

One year after the publication of my first book and some months after a *Miami Herald* interview about it, I received an email I had under the name of Fernando that said, "Hi Ella, I admire your courage. I am glad that you found yourself. I would never have believed it. I hope you have a great time, and I remain your friend." This email came from an ex-colleague and longtime friend, and it changed everything.

The first thing I did was to officially make sure that Fernando was gone from social media. Fernando's Facebook page disappeared, and my LinkedIn was changed. I made an informal statement about my transition to friends and business acquaintances. The reaction was overwhelming. Many emails and messages came in with similar contents, such things as, "I am proud of you," "I admire you for your courage," and "You are the best." There were also many people that remained silent, though I had expected the opposite.

The first real proof that I was passable in my new gender was the first time I attended a trade show, one of those places where everybody knows each other.

It was the day of setting up the booths for the exhibition. My team had finished, and I decided to make a small walk around. It did not take long for me to see someone I knew from my past life. I wondered if I should move past this person in stealth mode or reintroduce myself. As I walked in his direction, he was clearly looking at me, so I just said, "Hi, how are you doing, Larry?"

He looked at her in a really shocked way and said, "Well, well, well, I would not recognize you, except for the voice. You do have a very special accent." And he laughed in a very friendly manner, so I laughed with him. "So what is your name now? I heard about you; the whole trade knows about you and what you did."

"My name is now Manuela."

"I really admire your courage. Wow, it takes a lot of *cojones* to do what you did," said Larry.

"I take that as a compliment, thank you."

"Well, we have heard of Caitlyn Jenner, but I would never have imagined that such a thing would hit so close to home."

"Well, you know that there are a lot of people like me. I suppose in the US alone about a million or so," I said.

"Ready for the new show?" he asked. "I am sure many people will come and visit you."

I was grateful that Larry shifted from the topic of my transition to the trade show. It suggested to me that he was entirely comfortable with who I was. "Yes, we are ready," I said and carried on talking about the business, how was it going, and so on.

Coming Home to Venus

Over the three days of the exhibition, I saw many old colleagues from different companies and business acquaintances that came to see me. Most of them congratulated me on my change. There were not many negative attitudes, but there were some, and a couple would just go to the other side of the corridor to avoid me.

There was only one group of people that showed their negativity, a company down in South that employed someone I had known and thought was a friend for a number of years. Since I had my own company, I had tried to sell them things without much result. They always had excuses not to buy, but there was a good relationship there.

"Hi, E. How are you doing?" I greeted them. "I would like to tell you in person about my transition since you are a person that always meant a lot to me."

"Hi, how are you doing?" he said without really looking at me.

At the same time his boss came over near and said, "Hi, Fernando, well, you look better than before."

"Well, my name is now Manuela," I gently corrected him.

"For me you will always be Fernando. It does not matter how you look. But how have your customers been taking you with your changes?"

I noticed the negativity coming in my direction, and I decided to give them a big smile and leave. There was nothing more to say. The three years that I had tried to bring them new technology and interesting upgrades to their production line had been a waste of time and never produced anything positive, so it was time to stop. The contact was broken, but it was the only one. Yes, there were people who were very nice in front of me and quite negative behind my back, but those were not the right people for the business or my personal growth.

All in all, the reception of the people important to me at this trade show was very positive, and my good contacts with existing customers and partners continued. But my goal was not to be only based on the old but to develop new ones, and for those, there was no discrimination. I was a woman, and taken like a woman.

On the private side of the life it was a time of discovery. I met many people that I became friends with, and I learned many things about myself and about my environment from them. Sure, I had my share of not so positive experiences, but that is part of life, and the positive outnumbered the negative by far.

One of the great experiences from that time was with one of my best friends, Missy. We had a great time together, great discussions, and during my divorce Missy was a great moral support. Soon after a third companion joined our group, a beautiful Swiss lady, Jane. Missy, Jane, and I used to spend a lot of together. Jane and Missy became very good friends during Hurricane Irma in Florida, and I joined them just after the storm passed.

One day Jane asked me, "So Manuela when are you going to get your boobs done?"

"I am not sure. I am not certain if I want to do them. After all my natural ones are C's, so it is not really necessary, but this is not my final decision. What about you? I know Missy has already had them done."

"I have an appointment with Dr. Cute in a couple of weeks," said Jane. "Hope all these hurricane issues are over then."

"Yes, Dr. Cute is a great doctor," Missy said. "Believe me he did mine and I am really happy with the outcome. I had a special procedure because I had no breasts whatsoever, so I had temporary implants where I was injecting a solution to build size, and then he put the final ones. So I actually had two surgeries, but the last one was a fast recovery."

"Yes, I remember that," I said. "I was partly taking care of you after the second surgery. Okay, if we are talking about surgeries, what about SRS?"

"No, no, no, *G*RS, *gender* reassignment surgery," said Jane. "That is the right name. We are reassigning our gender to fit our brain. Well, that is on my wish list; it is a definitive must for me. I want to be a complete woman."

"Me too," said Missy. "The question is when and by whom."

"For me, too, sisters," I said. "I have been doing some research into this theme, and I think I would like to go to Thailand for this. After all they have the most experience. I will send you the website connection to Dr. Chettawut in Bangkok. He is very good, and I know someone that was operated on by him. We can talk to her; I am sure she has some tips. He has a complete different surgery method than the classical American system."

"Why do you want to go to Thailand? We have great doctors in the US," said Missy.

"Well, in South Florida there are two specialists. One is going to retire, and the other is a total disaster. I have friends that were operated on by him, and the results far from good. The only fantastic one is Dr. Bowers in San Francisco, but she has a waiting list of three years and the method is completely different from the ones in Thailand. There are some others as well, but we have to look at their experience."

"Yes, that is a real dream for me," Jane sighed. " Toe a complete woman, no excuses, no explanations."

"That would be great. We could all three of us go to Thailand and support each other," said Missy.

And like that, Pandora's box was open for gender reassignment surgery.

I had met Jessmarie, a young, very beautiful girl, around this time, and somehow, we connected right from the start. We talked a lot and became good friends. One day there was an event and an old friend of Jessmarie's from New York, Sebastian, appeared. Sebastian started to talk to me about where I came from, and there was an apparent interest there.

At the same time Sebastian was texting Jessmarie, "Is Manuela trans?"

Jessmarie answered, "Yes, she is."

He did not want to believe this, and he carried on talking to me.

Coming Home to Venus

As it turned out Sebastian was a leading person in a kind of religious community.

Religion and spirituality were something that always attracted me. When I was young it was the Catholic church; later I was very attracted to different religions and spiritual cults, such as Hinduism, Buddhism, Candomblé and others. I never became a member but rather someone who learned about these religions and tried to understand them. Somehow I always felt very close to the various entities and prayed to them, but since I had been in a Catholic school at a very young age I had an aversion to the religious organizations that were taking advantages of people.

Within weeks of meeting Sebastian, I started to enter the religion that he practiced. Sebastian was a brilliant scholar, very intelligent and persuasive, and I was impressed.

I talked with him about my grandfather's book, *Africa Bantu*, which was written in 1938 about the sub-Saharan African cultures. It is an anthropological book about African tribes, the ways they lived, their religions, their languages and culture in general that is still a reference book in all major universities in the world for African culture. This triggered a lot of ideas and communication between us and somehow helped me to be initialized into his religion.

"Manuela, I would like to invite you to a gathering. I think you will like it a lot," Sebastian said one day.

"Yes. It is so interesting that there are so many common points between this religious practice and my past and my family's past. I am really interested to know more about it and to understand it."

"We are going to meet next Saturday. I will send you all the information," he said.

The Saturday came, and the ceremony took place in a private house. That did not surprise me at all; some years before I had been invited by another religious movement called the Baha'i and all the ceremonies were held in private houses. I learned a lot about this fantastic religion and about the struggles of its followers, many of them of Iranian origin, who were subject to being followed and killed by their Islamic religious government. It is one of the biggest religious tragedies of our times. The Baha'i community in South Florida is quite incredible.

Coming back to our ceremony, Jessmarie and many people that I called friends were there. I was very fascinated by it, and it was a fantastic experience. Everybody sat down in a circle, and there were prayers and some specific rituals to this religion. There was a word or a gesture for every single person present. I thought I was in the right place and carried out this experience. I went to quite a lot of these meetings and ceremonies until one day, due to a multitude of issues, it all stopped for me. While there were many interesting and strong experiences in this religion, it was time for me to carry on my journey somewhere else.

Jessmarie and I are not only friends but sisters in religion, a friendship that with time has had its highs and its lows but survives to this day.

Yes, a new life was taking shape; a new degree of independence and freedom was setting in; there were new experiences and new journeys, but there was an important point that I was still missing: my gender reassignment surgery.

Coming Home to Venus

The Final Step to Venus

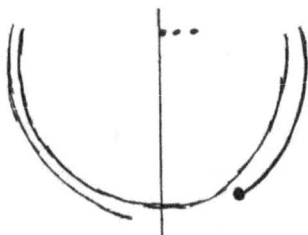

"Simply stated, our bodies and mind are closely connected, and that which affects our state of mind will invariably affect the way in which our bodies function."

Margaret Cuomo

The idea of the three of us going to Thailand and having our surgeries at the same time had been broken.

One day Missy and I got a text from Jane: "Thought I had a cold, but the doctor sent me to the hospital in Sarasota, apparently I have cancer."

We immediately took the car and went to visit our friend in the hospital.

"Hi, what is going on, girl?" I asked.

"Yes, how are you feeling?" said Missy.

"Well, you know I thought I had the flu, so I went to the doctor. He told me there was something not right and he told me to go the hospital to have it checked. I got there, they did some checks and told me I had to stay there. Since they could not find a place for me, they sent me here with an ambulance. They diagnosed me with cancer, leukemia, so here I am. I will have chemo tomorrow."

"Oh my God, just like that without warning," said Missy.

"Yes, I had no idea—well I was starting to have bruises on my body, but I never thought it was that bad. "

"Life is full of unknowns. It's incredible what can happen from one day to the other," I said.

"So I am asking my health insurance what to do, you know I still have Swiss health insurance. In the meantime the doctor here told me I needed an urgent leukemia treatment."

"Oh my God, I wish you all the best, sister. You always looked so healthy, it is hard to believe," I said.

"And you know, since I am trans, they could not put me in a women's ward or a men's room so I have my own private room, I like it" said Jane.

It was the last time we saw her for some time. The Swiss health system sent a private jet with doctors and nurses, and she was moved to Switzerland. I visited her in Switzerland two years later; she is still fighting but much better.

With Jane gone there were only two people to take the surgery together, and we really missed Jane. Missy and I carried on studying different surgeons. There were many, but somehow the Thailand connection seemed to be the best option. The biggest concern was that, if something happened, it was a very long trip to go back. Many people were talking about the quality of Thai surgeons compared to US ones, and the more we looked, the more we were convinced about Thailand. There were many factors to the final choice, but the first was the procedure itself. The Thai procedure seemed to both of us the most adequate. The procedure in Thailand is based on a non-penile inversion system,[xvi] whereas in the US the standard system uses penile inversion,[xvii] with Dr. Bowers in San Francisco having the best reputation.

 The second was that we knew people in Florida that had had the same surgery with the same Thai doctor and were very happy. There was no need to go back in all the cases.

And the third was the experience that this surgeon had. He had performed thousands of identical surgeries, and most of his patients never had to return.

"So Missy, what is your decision? Are you convinced about Dr. Chettawut?" I asked one day.

"Yes, I am, but I just want to hear from this doctor in C Clinic. The good thing about him is that my health insurance would cover it and in Thailand I would have to pay myself."

"I can understand that. Did he tell you how many such surgeries he has done?" I asked.

"No, that is the information I am waiting for."

A couple of days later, Missy texted me. "Girl, this guy has only done some thirty surgeries, let's go to Thailand."

Well, that was the beginning of some big, big changes. First was the planning; we started to talk to Dawn, a girl who had operated on some years before by the good doctor. She was married to a Thai girl and went regularly to Thailand.

"You will see he is a great doctor," Dawn said. "He has lots of experience, and the care he gives you is nothing like an American doctor. You will be surprised."

"Oh, that sounds great. Where did you stay?" asked Missy.

"After surgery you will stay in the clinic for a couple of days; then you will go to a place where you will rest for about three weeks. A nurse comes every day to see you and see how are you improving. I recommend a place that is very nice; it specializes in this type of surgery. I was there myself. And I am sure you will not be the only patients of Dr. Chettawut who stay there."

"That sounds really interesting, so these people are really organized for such things?" I asked.

"Yes, they are, and another thing: this place has cottages, so you guys can go out and walk in plain air when you feel better. You will see, it is a great place. They also have a good restaurant and a supermarket nearby."

She was a real help, and with all of her information and contacts, we were ready to go. We each got an appointment for the surgery. Mine was set for Valentine's Day and Missy's was for the following day, so with the time difference it was technically Valentine's Day in the US for both of us. With the booking, we both made a down payment and received a list of tests to be done for final approval for the surgery. This list was quite standard: blood tests, an electrocardiogram, lung X-rays, and so on. It was very common for a pre-op evaluation, but this time there was also a heart stress test. The other requirements were as usual the psychiatrist letters, two of them, according to WPATH.[xviii]

I went to my doctor, who at the time was a woman called Sherryl.

"Hi, Dr. Sherryl. I made a decision, and I am going to have my gender reassignment surgery done."

"Oh, nice to hear that, that is a big step. So who is going to be the surgeon?"

"I am going to Thailand and I have chosen Dr. Chettawut. He has a fantastic track record, and I think he is the right person to do it."

"I have heard about him. He seems to be a very good doctor, but I have to remind everybody that he is far away and if there are any issues, it could be a problem."

"I know. It was always a large concern. When I decided to go with him, I asked and did some homework and I have to say that only a very small part of people actually had issues. We are talking about two or three in thousands of surgeries he has performed. And sometimes one has to take a risk. I prefer a good doctor, distance is for me less an issue, than experience."

"Okay, well I wish you all the best. So how can I help you?"

Dr. Sherryl did or referred me out for all the tests, and I had an appointment with a cardiologist for the stress test.

"Hi, my name is Manuela Marques. I have an appointment with the cardiologist," I said at Dr. Tim's office.

Soon I was escorted to a room, where I waited for Dr. Tim.

"Hi, you are Manuela," said Dr. Tim with a clear Latino accent. "So, your GP said you should perform a stress test, but I do not see what the reason is. Ban you explain?"

"Sure, I am a transgender woman, I decided to have my SRS done, and the surgeon is asking for this test."

"Okay, please explain, I didn't understand."

"Okay," I said, steeling myself for yet another conversation about my gender identity. "I am a transgender woman."

"Transgender woman, what do you mean?"

"Well, I was born a boy and I am becoming a girl. You know what a transgender person is?"

"Yes, yes, of course now I get it, but why do you want the stress test?"

"Well I am going to do an SRS, meaning a sex reassignment surgery, and the surgeon requests this test."

"Oh, and where are you going to do the surgery?" asked Dr. Tim

"In Thailand, with Dr. Chettawut. He is one of the best doctors for this procedure."

"I see, but why do you want to get this type of surgery?"

At that moment I was running out of patience. Why would a cardiologist ask such questions> It was none of his business. Why should I start something that I already had gone through for so many years? So I said, "Dr. Tim, I just need the stress test. I have been going through a series of specialists to answer all those questions and the answer is very simple: I want to be a complete woman. It's my life and my understanding."

Apparently that was enough for Dr. Tim. "Okay, just a second," he said and left the room. Soon after an assistant came, and they performed an electrocardiogram on me. I had to wait for the doctor again.

"Based on the results of the electrocardiogram I have no reason to send you for a stress test," he told me. "I understand that you need it for your surgery, so I am going to send the information to your health insurance and they will let you know when it can be done and if they will pay for it."

It took another two weeks until a letter from my health insurance came to tell me that the stress test was not covered; I had good health and I didn't need it. I got in touch with the cardiologist's office and asked where I could get this test done. After many telephones and discussions, they sent a referral to go to a cardiologist institute.

At the institute, one of the nurses had some news I had already anticipated. "Your insurance is telling that they are not paying for this procedure," they said. "Sorry, why do you want to have this anyway?"

"I need it for some plastic surgery, my surgeon is asking for it." This was the answer I had figured out got me through enough doors. "Is there a possibility to do it privately? How much does it cost?"

"I will have to see. Please take a seat, I will come back to you."

After an hour, they told me the test would cost $1,800 unless I went online and asked for a low-income petition.

I thanked them and went home. I wrote to Dr. Chettawut's office with an update on everything, and the next morning I got a simple answer: "If you cannot get the stress test it will not be an issue. Please send all the other tests and you will take the stress test here in Thailand before the operation. The price is sixty US dollars."

And that is exactly what I did. I got all the other tests together, sent them all in with the two letters from my counselors, and I was ready to go. The two WPATH letters were not difficult to get; I went to Dr. Clark and to Lisa, another counselor I had been seeing for almost a year, a fantastic counselor that helped me in many respects to discover myself.

Missy had no issues getting her tests and paperwork; somehow her doctors were easier to deal with. We booked a small cottage room for the recovery and our flights.

Finally the day came to go on our new adventure. We flew from Fort Lauderdale to JFK in New York; then on to Seoul, a fourteen-and-a-half-hour flight; and finally to Bangkok, another six hours. The total flight time was almost twenty four hours, and that didn't include the waiting time at the airports. We arrived in Bangkok completely exhausted.

The service of Dr. Chettawut started to show immediately; there was a driver picking us up from the airport and driving us to the hotel. The next day we went to the doctor's clinic to enter all of our information and get ready for our surgeries. We had arrived several days early to make sure that we were rested and in good form. The day for the stress test was defined, and all was organized.

On the morning of the test, two nurses were waiting for me in the lobby.

"Hi, Manuela, we are taking you now to hospital for the stress test," said one of the nurses.

"Thank you, you are really well organized," I said.

We drove for about half an hour in one of the cities that must have had the worst traffic that I have ever seen. It was very difficult to get around. Then we arrived at this very modern-looking and beautiful hospital. One of the nurses drove the car to the garage while the other went with me inside. We walked to the main desk and the rest of the conversation was in Thai; I could not understand. We were told to sit down and wait. After some moments a nurse from the hospital came and took me to a testing room. They took my blood, and I went back to the waiting room.

I had some difficulty talking to the nurses; one had a very broken English and the other hardly spoke anything of English. Soon after they took me to another floor where I had an electrocardiogram, and then the famous stress electrocardiogram. This is just an electrogram on a walking machine from the gym. I hardly see how it costs $1,800 back in Florida. I went out again to the waiting room for quite a prolonged time, and then I had to go and see a local doctor.

"Hi, how do you feel?" asked the doctor.

"I feel great," I said.

"Here are all your tests. You are perfectly healthy. Your blood values are good; the electrocardiogram, lung X-rays, and stress test all are perfect."

"I am glad. I thought so."

"Which leads me to the next question: Why did you do all these tests? Is there a specific reason?"

"Oh, you do not know. These tests are pre-op tests for my sex reassignment surgery," I said.

It dropped like a bomb; the doctor was looking at me with his mouth wide open.

"I don't understand."

One of the nurses started to explain to him about my surgery and why we were there. The poor doctor looked like the world had come to an end; apparently, he was quite shocked.

"Well, Manuela, I would never had guessed. You look so feminine. I understand now. Good luck with the procedure."

After that, with all the results in the hands of the nurses, they drove me back to the hotel. The crazy stress test that cost a fortune in the US was done, I had passed with flying colors, and the surgery could take place. I thought, 'Oh my God, in Thailand a test like this does not cost almost anything. There is definitely an issue with the American health system. My lab work usually takes one week until it is finished, here not even a day, and it seems to be the same as far as machines and procedures are concerned. Incredible.'

The next days, waiting for the surgery, Missy and I visited the fantastic city of Bangkok. What a great culture! The food was really impressive. We took advantage also of the opportunity to get prepared for life immediately post- surgery, like having enough food in the room. It was not really a good room for cooking, but there was enough to make tea and some basic things. We would get breakfast and most food from the hotel, and we found very soon that one could get food and supermarket deliveries anytime, using some great phone apps. We were ready to go.

Coming Home to Venus

I was the first. The day came, after a difficult twenty-four hours of purging my stomach on a prescribed liquid diet. Again I was picked up from the hotel and driven to the clinic of Dr. Chettawut. When I arrived I was escorted to a room on the first floor, stripped naked and prepared for the intervention with the usual blue surgery open dresses, and was waiting there for some hours in a comfortable special room .

Suddenly the door opened, the nurse came in and said, "Manuela, how do you feel? It's your time. You are going to become the woman you always wanted to be. Ready?"

"Yes, I am ready." Wow after so many years and dreams I was finally going to be complete. But there was as well a lot of fears, what if something goes wrong? It was time for the truth.

"Come on, let's go then." The nurse took me to the room next door. I had already been given quite a lot of medication, so I was not really in a position to walk. I was taken to the next room on a rolling bed. The room next door was an operating theater; there, they transferred me to the operating table. There were a couple of people waiting for me; one was Dr. Chettawut, and then there was the anesthetist that I recognized as the person who had driven us from the airport to the hotel. There were also two nurses, all having on very clean and safe surgical gear.

"Ready for the change, Manuela?" asked Dr. Chettawut.

"Ready as I can be."

"Okay, I am going to give you an injection and you are going to have sweet dreams," said the anesthetist as he injected me with some medicine. It did not take long for me to be knocked out.

Later, I was slowly waking up. I opened my eyes. I had no pain, but I could not move either. Slowly my vision cleared, and I tried to see what was going on. The last memories I had were in the operating room. Soon I could see I was back in the prep room. I moved her head; it was not easy but slowly I was coming back to life.

Very soon a nurse came in.

"Hello, Miss Manuela, how do you feel after your birth?" she said. "The surgery went well. There were great results, as you will see soon. It took eight and a half hours."

"Hi," I think I murmured. I was not quite awake.

"You are still under the influence of the anesthesia, so you should not have much pain. We will transfer you to your room very soon."

Soon I was transferred to another room in the same clinic. It was a regular room with some kind of central television surveillance so that I could be seen at all times by the nurses. I have no idea of the time, but at some point I woke up. This time the pain was pretty high. The pain was between the legs and in my butt. This was no wonder after all that surgery time on my butt. I tried to move with a lot of pain, and within a couple of minutes there was a nurse in the room.

"Hi, Miss Manuela, how are you feeling?" said the nurse.

"It hurts, but mostly in my bum."

"That is normal. We have some painkillers for you, see if you can take them."

The nurse gave me a pill followed by some water. I took the pill and drank the water, but it did not take one minute for me to start vomiting. There was the little that she had in her stomach, but it was out, all over the bed.

"Oh, you cannot take opioids," the nurse said with a tsk. Within a couple of minutes, another nurse came in, and both of them cleaned everything and changed my bed sheets.

My first days in the clinic were full of pain, but I have no regrets. After three days my butt was still bruised and hurting, but I got to see my new parts. It was a huge change, but I had many different feelings. One was the pain. I could take no painkillers except some Tylenol; the other was happiness. Sheer bliss.

Yes, I was finally on Venus. I was a girl in every aspect of my being. I started to walk, so it was time to go to the hotel and rest there. Missy had the same surgery, and a similar experience. All was taken care with the help of our angel nurse. For the next few weeks, I felt like I was the most important person in the world, and what a job she did making me feel that way.

Coming Home to Venus

Opening to the New World, Being on Venus

"Coming out of your comfort zone is tough in the beginning,
chaotic in the middle, and awesome in the end...because in
the end, it shows you a whole new world !!
Make an attempt.."
Manoj Arora,

I returned to the hotel room, still in pain, but it was getting better every day. The first night I was alone, and I managed to take care of myself quite well. The next day Missy came to the room; as you can expect, she was tired and in a lot of pain.

"Hi sister, how do you feel?" I asked.

"Doing better, still on some painkillers. The surgery went on for approximately nine hours, but my butt hurts a lot," said Missy.

"Well, girl, same surgery, same symptoms," I said.

During our time in the hotel, Missy and I helped each other heal, and we both became more autonomous on a daily basis. As soon as my catheter was removed, there was more freedom of movement, and we started to venture outside for short walks. Soon we met all the girls who had also had surgery with Dr. Chettawut. The doctor performed about one surgery per day, and there were girls from Australia, England, Dubai, all over the world having the same procedure. Most of them were not alone; some had friends with them, and I must say we understood why. Things like food and groceries were delivered to the room, but a good helping hand was always welcome. The nurses would come every day at the same time to see how we were, to look at the progress, and to help us with dilation. That was certainly a new experience. In the beginning it was very painful and had to be done on a regular basis to make sure that your new organs were kept in the right shape and size. Out of some seven girls in the hotel that had the same procedure done, only one had a small issue, and the doctor corrected this immediately. We started to be friends with some of them, Elisa was an English woman, Charlese was from Australia, other girls were from Slovakia, there was an Indian girl, well it was like the united nations.

"Yes, I am very happy with the outcome. My surgery was about eight hours, and I think I can feel the quality of work that was done," said Elisa.

"Yes, mine was a similar time, and I think it is getting better and better," I said.

"I am not sure when the doctor sleeps. He does one surgery a day, and they are long surgeries. He has also has patients coming in all the time for consults, he is really incredible," said Missy.

"Yes, he is incredible. I was asking a surgeon in the UK how long the surgery would be and he told me about three to four hours," said Elisa.

"Wow, that is big difference. Why does he take longer than the others?" said Charlene, another woman at the hotel.

"I am not sure, but I heard from a girl back in the US that the quality and length of the stitching is much better. That is why he has great results, but it takes longer to operate," I said.

"What strikes me as well is that we are all so different, from all ages and backgrounds, and from all over the world," Elisa said with a smile.

After many doctor's visits and follow-ups, both Missy and I were doing much better. We could walk, even if with some pain, and were discharged.

Coming Home to Venus

The trip back to Florida again took approximately twenty-four hours, with wheelchairs in every airport. It was not a fun trip; we both felt like we were literally finished, but we survived. Mainly the last stop in New York was the most difficult; both of us were just completely tired.

Back in Florida, it was a challenge to get back into my usual rhythm, so I did not take as many business trips. Instead I had a good time of rehabilitation. The only issues for me were the hormones. I had stopped taking hormones one month before the surgery and restarted one month after the surgery, so in total I spent about two months without hormones. When I restarted, I had many issues with hot flashes and then freezing shivers. My body was very irregular, like a thermostat was going crazy. This lasted only some two or three days, and then all went back to normal. During this period, there was a lot of hormonal fluctuation that led to a lot of weight gain.

Slowly my life went back to normal, but it was not an easy time. Beyond my transition, there were some challenges and some great times in this period of my life.

My daughter Victoria was working at a gallery in north Miami that belonged to one of my best friends, Bianca, a great Brazilian girl with an incredible culture, a lot of energy, and a fantastic international touch. We had gone to the same school in Switzerland but not at the same time; instead we met at one of the school reunions and immediately became friends. Since my office was not too far from the gallery, we were together very often. Bianca was always there with Victoria when she had issues, to help her.

One very happy note was Victoria's marriage to her high school sweetheart, Tommy. They make a great couple.

"Oi, Papi," Victoria said to me over the phone one day. That was the name she always called me. "Let me know if you can come on Wednesday to look at the wedding dress. I am trying some on, and I would like to know what you think."

"Of course, Victoria, I will be there," I said. "That is such a great compliment that you want me to come. Where is it?"

"It is in Boca Raton, I will text you the address and the time."

"That is great. I am looking forward to seeing what you choose. I am sure it will be beautiful. What kind of dress do you want, a ballroom type or a mermaid dress?"

"You will see. I am just not so sure about the accessories, and mainly I would like to have a lace top, though I'm not sure how it should look. I find them so beautiful."

"Yes, they are," I agreed.

"Also, Tommy and I would love to have an arch for our wedding. Do you think you could find one?"

"Sure, I can see what I can find."

I started to look for a suitable arch online. There were a thousand suitable ones, but somehow they were not the right one. It had to be one that was simple, in real wood, that could be nicely decorated with flowers. Well I was no stranger to woodwork, so I decided to make one myself. I went to Home Depot, bought some first-class oak, and made a quite beautiful one in my garden. Thank God it was not raining during this time. The only challenge was the transportation, but I drove a white Mustang convertible at the time that I called the "convertible pickup" because when the top was down there was quite a lot of storage space.

The day came to see the gown, and Victoria just looked so beautiful. This dress was strapless, column type showing just how perfect she was, and it had a train. It was simple and beautiful in immaculate white.

"What do you think?" asked Victoria. Her mother was present as well, and it was the first time I had seen her since we moved out of the house in Boca.

"Well, girl, I see that you already found something absolutely stunning, and you look gorgeous in it. What a bride," I said.

"Yes, now I need some accessories for it: a lace top and a diamond belt—well, not real ones." She laughed.

"Yes, I probably have something for you," said the shop attendant and left to get them.

When we were left alone, Victoria turned to me. "Papi, you are walking me down the aisle, right?"

"Of course, my love. Let me know what I should wear. Do you want me to go as a man?" I asked. I would do anything for her, even the worst thing I could imagine.

"No! You should come as your beautiful self. Just bring a nice- one colored dress, not too fancy or showy."

"Sure, I will find something that is suitable for you, probably in dark blue, since that is more neutral."

"Try this small jacket, Victoria," said the shop attendant. "I just need to know the exact date when you are getting married because we will have to make one for you." Victoria tried this little jacket along with some different tops and belts.

"What about shoes? What are you wearing?" I asked.

"The ones I am wearing now, I think they look good with it," said Victoria, showing some nice, light beige heels.

"I see that you have everything organized and thought of. You are amazing, Victoria," I said, and everyone agreed.

I had to find a dress for Victoria's wedding, which was not an easy thing. In South Florida people are spoilt with buying nice things; there are lots of incredible shops and shopping centers, so I went to the biggest one in South Florida. After hours and hours of looking, I found something I thought was suitable in one of the haute couture stores. It was a royal blue dress, slightly fitted but beautiful, the right length and not low-cut. I tried it on, and it fit quite well, so I sent a photo to Victoria and got a very positive reply with the usual question, "What shoes are you going to wear?" That was taken care of as well with some nice, not too high heels in beige.

Coming Home to Venus

The day of the wedding I got up early, delivered, and assembled the arch at the beach outside the restaurant where the ceremony would take place and went back home. At the right time I went back. The flower people were there to arrange everything, the guests were going to a room to have some drinks, and as typical on such an occasion, the stress to make everything perfect for everybody was there, giving the place a sense of total chaos. It all turned out better than perfect, even though there was some rain expected and the ceremony would be outside.

It was a really small but perfect family wedding. Only the close family came, no friends. Victoria intended to have a bigger wedding party one or two years later. The Marques side was definitely a minority, but my son David and his very pregnant wife, Gaby, came all the way from Switzerland. All the family sat outside, the organizers gave the sign that Victoria and I could start walking, and we did.

"You look magnificent, my daughter," I said, giving her my hand as we walked down the aisle.

"Thank you, Papi, I am so nervous."

"I can understand, but don't be. Everything is going to go just great."

I walked Victoria down the aisle and gave her to Tommy, and they got married under the wooden arch that was magnificently decorated with white flowers. Tears of happiness were sprouting up all over the place.

After the wedding, we all sat at different tables in the reception hall. There were speeches and it was a great day, and we were all so happy for the newlyweds.

The next day, Gaby, Victoria, and I went for lunch together. David had left already to Switzerland, and his wife was going back a bit later.

So the most important question popped up. "Gaby, do you know what it is going to be, a boy or a girl?" asked Victoria.

The answer was short but probably one of the most moving I had ever heard. "Yes, I know, but I will not tell at the moment. We chose a neutral name that is good for both genders, if it is a boy or a girl. This way, he or she will not have to change their name later if it is transgender."

Wow, I was taken away by my tears. Some months later a boy came into the world and soon after I went to meet my first grandson in Switzerland. It was love at first sight. I was convinced that these two were fantastic parents taking great care of their little love.

Coming Home to Venus

On the same trip, I visited my friend Jane. She was still on her way to recovery, after almost two years of leukemia treatment, but she was doing better. We exchanged all the details of the surgery and what had happened in both of our lives. I still regretted that Jane had missed out on Thailand.

Yes, I had fully transitioned, become a grandmother, had two of my three children now married, and a third wedding probably on the way. Yes, big changes had taken place, but life is an eternal change, and transgender people have some additional issues to face that are just a part of normal life.

It is not a choice to be transgender. We are born this way, and somehow our body does not match our brain. Many researchers have studied the transgender brain.[xix] The structure of the male and female brain is different, and these studies came to the conclusion that most transgender people have a brain that is identical or similar to their identity, not to the gender they were assigned at birth. Well, it is the brain that guides you and not your sexual parts, which probably explains why to be transgender is not a choice, it is a reality.

Most transgender people would love to be recognized as such from the time they know they are transgender, meaning at a very early age. In my case I was no older than five. Probably if I could have taken a brain scan then it would have been clear that I was transgender, and all could have been done appropriately—school, clothes, career. If society would accept that as the truth, the world would be a much better place.

I don't think that most people realize what transgender people go through in their lives; no one has an easy path. There always have been struggles along the way. Some decide to stop it with suicide; many fight all their lives against themselves. Only few arrive at a stage where they can say they are complete and happy.

Unfortunately, transgender people have many enemies. There is no mention in the Bible of transgender people being evil! This is only made up by some extremist groups, in some religions. In others there are even transgender gods. Discrimination against transgender people in the US is increasing with the evangelical rise to power that is taking place in this country, and that is putting many years of progress for transgender people, for women, and for the gay, bisexual, lesbian immigrants and people of color communities at risk. Well, it is not the first time that something like this has happened in the history of mankind and it will not be the last. Even so, transgender people have always existed, if governments like it or not.

Discrimination is a big issue for transgender people. I have never had open problems with discrimination, but behind my back I know that many people talk about me in a negative way. As far as business is concerned, I believe that people do not care about my gender, but sometimes I am not sure.

Like everything in life, one has to be at peace with oneself to be at peace with the world. Some people have an easier time of arriving at this than others. Transgender people sometimes have to fight long and hard to arrive at the true recognition of themselves, so why should we also have to fight against a society that tries to criminalize us? Transgender people are just people. Acceptance is what we ask for.

My biggest wish for the future, like most people on the planet, is to be happy. For me this means that my business is working with no major issues, that I will not be discriminated against, in business or otherwise. I hope that I can share my life with my loved ones, my family, my friends, and who knows, maybe someday a special person. I hope that my health will continue to be good. By writing books and recording internet videos I am sharing with the community and I am not keeping my identity a secret. Yes, I know many transgender people that live in stealth mode, meaning that they don't tell people that they are transgender. I admire them and I think they should do what they feel is best for them. I have chosen to speak up for this community. I admire you all with your struggles, sometimes to come out, sometimes about being perfect or not, but I encourage you to remember that beauty is always in the eye of the beholder. We should never forget that. Look toward the future. I know it is not easy for anybody, but follow your inner self, your feelings, be positive, work hard, and I pray that someday the world will be with you.

References

[i] Dr. Carol Clark is a board-certified sex therapist and addictions counselor, as well as president and senior instructor for Therapy Certification Training, the International Transgender Certification Association, and the International Institute of Clinical Sexology.

[ii] Clark, Carol. *Addict America.* Amazon Services LLC, 2011.

[iii] "The Harry Benjamin International Gender Dysphoria Association was the first professional group to form and write up standards on how to go about treating transgender patients. This association has since been renamed the World Professional Association for Transgender Health (WPATH)." Teich, Nicholas. *Transgender 101* (New York: Columbia University Press, 2012), 56.

[iv] The eligibility criteria for adults to begin hormone therapy. Retrieved from Teich, *Transgender 101*, 56.

[v] "Hair removal by electrolysis, plucking, or waxing can be extremely detrimental to your recovery." Ousterhout, Douglas. *Facial Feminization Surgery: A Guide for the Transgendered Woman* (Omaha, NE: Addicus Books, 2010), 115.

[vi] Song, Martine. *How to Feminize Your Voice*. Amazon Services LLC, 2019.

[vii] Perez, Kathe. "Voice Feminization." Exceptional Voice. www.exceptionalvoice.com/voice-feminization/.

[viii] Ousterhout, *Facial Feminization.*

[ix] "Sex change surgery is a life-changing decision." Retrieved from Nye, Eleanor. *Sex Change - Male to Female: An Essential Guide*

for *Understanding the Process of Gender Reassignment Surgery & Getting to Know the New You* (Amazon Services LLC, 2015).

[x] "Breast augmentation, also known as 'augmentation mammoplasty….'" Retrieved from Goldschmidt, Matt. *The Great Book of Boobs: Everything You Need to Know about Breast Augmentation* (Phoenix, AZ: Jones Media Publishing, 2017).

[xi] https://www.lgbtmap.org/mapping-trans-equality

[xii] "ID Documents Center | Florida." National Center for Transgender Equality. 2020. https://transequality.org/documents/state/florida.

[xiii] "Home." Transgender Network Switzerland. 2020. www.tgns.ch/de/.

[xiv] "National Transgender Discrimination Survey." National Center for Transgender Equality. September 11, 2012. https://transequality.org/issues/resources/national-transgender-discrimination-survey-full-report.

[xv] "The Discrimination Administration." National Center for Transgender Equality. 2020. https://transequality.org/the-discrimination-administration.

[xvi] "Concept of Male to Female Sex Reassignment Surgery." Chettawut Plastic Surgery Center. 2019. www.chet-plasticsurgery.com/sex-reassignment-surgery/.

[xvii] "History and Procedure." Marci L. Bowers, M.D. 2020. https://marcibowers.com/transfem/gav/history-procedure/.

[xviii] WPATH Standards of Care Version 7. World Professional Association for Transgender Health. 2020. www.wpath.org/publications/soc.

[xix] "Research on the Transgender Brain: What You Should Know." Cleveland Clinic. March 27, 2019. https://health.clevelandclinic.org/research-on-the-transgender-brain-what-you-should-know/.

www.ingramcontent.com/pod-product-compliance
Lightning Source LLC
Chambersburg PA
CBHW031156270326
41931CB00006B/289